Practical Buddhism:

living everyday life

PRACTICAL BUDDHISM

living everyday life

by

KENNETH LIBERMAN, PhD

Foreword by

VEN. THUBTEN CHODRON

MOTILAL BANARSIDASS PUBLISHERS
PRIVATE LIMITED • DELHI

First Edition: ***Delhi, 2016***

ISBN: 978-81-208-4024-9

MOTILAL BANARSIDASS
41 U.A. Bungalow Road, Jawahar Nagar, Delhi 110 007
8 Mahalaxmi Chamber, 22 Bhulabhai Desai Road, Mumbai 400 026
203 Royapettah High Road, Mylapore, Chennai 600 004
236, 9th Main III Block, Jayanagar, Bengaluru 560 011
8 Camac Street, Kolkata 700 017
Ashok Rajpath, Patna 800 004
Chowk, Varanasi 221 001

MLBD Cataloging-in-Publication Data
Practical Buddhism
living everyday life
by KENNETH LIBERMAN
ISBN: 978-81-208-4024-9
I. Buddhism II. Liberman, Kenneth
III. Chodron, Ven. Thubten

Printed in India

by RP Jain at NAB Printing Unit,
A-44, Naraina Industrial Area, Phase I, New Delhi–110028
and published by JP Jain for Motilal Banarsidass Publishers (P) Ltd,
41 U.A. Bungalow Road, Jawahar Nagar, Delhi-110007

Foreword

by Ven Thubten Chodron

Ken Liberman and I initially met in 1978 at Kopan Monastery, outside of Kathmandu, Nepal, where we were attending a one-month meditation course taught by Lama Thubten Yeshe, and Lama Zopa Rinpoche. Both of us were been deeply touched by the Buddha's teachings and wanted to learn and practice more. In addition, Lama Yeshe's skillful presentation of the teaching hooked us. Lama had the uncanny ability to speak the harsh truth about our personal and societal confusion in a way that got us to laugh at ourselves and at the same time see that this was a serious situation we needed to attend to.

Over the next few years, Ken and I kept bumping into each other at teachings and Dharma centers in India and Nepal, but after a while the "winds of karma" took us to different parts of the world. We both pursued our chosen Dharma paths, Ken as a serious lay practitioner, me as a monastic. Every few years we would run into each other at a Dharma event somewhere in the world and check in with each other. I've consistently admired Ken's ability to combine scholarship and practice, and his humility regarding his accomplishments in both. He has a wide variety of interests—including yoga, surfing, and Indian culture—and brings the perspectives gleaned from these to bear when he examines an issue. He lives a full life, having chosen to follow his heart rather than to fill his wallet, and I am constantly amazed how a Buddhist scholar who's had five heart surgeries can be so attached to surfing!

Ken has spent a quarter of his life living outside of the U.S., and many of these Dharma stories occurred abroad. His first international trip was to the southern Philippines when he was 19. His college had sent him to teach English to high school students in a Muslim village on the island of Mindanao. It was there that he first glimpsed people who were more contented with their lives than many of those where he grew up, in the affluent Los Angeles suburb of Beverly Hills. The warmth that the Filipino Muslims shared with each other in their streets and front porches each evening touched him deeply: they demonstrated an eagerness to know and care for each other that he sought but could not easily find when he returned home. Instead of a soft concern for one's neighbors, his Beverly Hills neighbors always seemed to be searching for something new and attractive. But ironically, they were much more dissatisfied than the Filipinos who owned much less. This triggered a strong resolve in Ken to quest for life's meaning, a journey that brought him to many corners of the world.

But he was not a tourist. He went to live with the most remote Aboriginal people of Australia, in the Central Desert, to learn how people without houses and who know only a natural landscape related to it. He learned their Pitjantjatjarra language and spent several years assisting them to secure their land rights. When I met him at Kopan in 1978, he had been deeply moved by the Buddhist notion of unbiased compassion and was also exploring the wisdom aspect of the path as well.

Although Lama Yeshe typically did not advise his students to learn the Tibetan language, he encouraged Ken to study it. Lama taught that Dharma practice is more important than scholarly knowledge, but Ken has sought ways to glean the practical from his philosophical investigations, which included European philosophers as well as Indian and Tibetan thinkers. He and his wife Anne went to Dharamsala, India, and after some time studying at the Library of Tibetan Works and Archives in the early

1980's, they went to Sakya College and the Dialectical Institute to pursue studies in more traditional Tibetan settings.

After Lama Yeshe passed away in 1984, Ken went to study with Lama's teachers at Sera Jey Monastic University in South India, where he spent several years studying the major texts on Madhyamaka philosophy. He has translated one text by the first Panchen Lama, and now brings study abroad students from the University of Oregon to spend a term studying there.

Ken now spends a good deal of time in Mexico and regularly travels to Argentina, Brazil, China, Denmark, India, and Italy to give short-term courses for graduate and postgraduate students of ethnomethodology. He still Professor Emeritus of Sociology at the University of Oregon, where he spent 30 years.

The anecdotes and reflections that Ken shares in *Practical Buddhism: living everyday life* are straight from his own life. Of course, each of us has grown up in different circumstances and encounters different situations in our lives, but no matter what culture or historical era we're from, our human minds function in very similar ways. Each of us wants to be happy and avoid suffering although different people, possessions, and places may bring us happiness or suffering. Despite this desire for happiness not misery, we lack the knowledge of what the causes for each are. In fact, we often find that the words we said or deeds we did with the conviction that they would bring us joy resulted in the opposite. The moment we get the gorgeous new car we've craved, we've entered "car hell," for the car will surely break down at the most inopportune times. The repairs will cost more than we like and may not completely fix the problem. Alongside "car hell" are situated "computer hell," "iPod and Blackberry hell," "relationship hell," and on and on. We keep looking outside of ourselves for someone or something that will bring us the satisfaction and joy we seek, yet these continually elude us. And to the contrary, the difficulties we shun find us anyway.

We're looking for happiness in the wrong place, like the famous story of the guy looking for his house key under the street lamp. "Where did you lose it?" asked a passerby, wanting to help the search. "On the other side of the street," said the man, "but it's dark over there and it's easier to look for it here where there's a street lamp."

Similarly, while the source of contentment and joy lie within ourselves, we exhaust ourselves trying to rearrange our environment so that everything we want is in it and everything we don't want has been expelled. But that's a fruitless pursuit because who amongst us is able to control the external world and everyone in it? We have lots of advice for how everyone else should live their lives so that we would be happy, but these people don't want to hear our advice and even if they do, they don't follow it correctly.

It would be wiser to look within our own hearts and minds and flesh out the wrong conceptions and fallacious expectations that prevent us from seeing things accurately. Our problem isn't that we can't get what we want, it's the craving itself. Based on an inflated idea of the goodness of someone or something, we crave it, telling ourselves there's no way we can possibly be happy without it. Meanwhile millions of other people live very well without that person or possession. Happiness doesn't abide in that person or object; happiness arises when we are free from obsessively craving it.

Similarly, misery does not abide in the person who harms us; misery arises from our self-centeredness and ignorance that skew our perception of that person. Another person does not make us angry; the seed of anger abides in our hearts and minds and until we uproot it, we will encounter "obnoxious" people and find people to hate wherever we go.

It would do us well to look inside and counteract the causes of suffering that are our misguided ways of thinking. This is what Buddhist practice is all about, and this is what Ken so accurately depicts in these revealing anecdotes. He shares his life with us, and through this we see our own lives. While the circumstances of his life may differ from ours, when we look past the external conditions to the human condition that lies behind them, we discover that we are all basically the same. Our anger may not arise when dealing with taxi drivers in India, but it may explode regarding our colleague at work who is delayed in completing a project that our work depends on. Our attachment may not be for a child's rubber ball, it may be for our reputation, but regardless, we share with the child a fixation on something that, at the end of the day, isn't very important because it has the nature of change. We may have grown up in a poor section of town, not in Beverly Hills, but family dynamics are similar; parents who are plagued with their own problems are trying to raise children as best they can despite their own physical, mental, and emotional limitations.

Read the book slowly, pausing after each chapter to contemplate its meaning and relate it to your own life. Extend understanding and compassion to yourself just as you do towards Ken as he reveals how he learns from life. Rejoice at your good qualities and virtues and know that your limitations are adventitious and can be eliminated. And remember that only we can do the work of eradicating them. While we can hire someone to fix our computers, only we can do the internal work necessary to "reformat" our way of thinking.

Enjoy the Dharma!

Bhikshuni Thubten Chodron
Sravasti Abbey
October 25, 2015

Contents

Acknowledgements

My teachers are now deceased. They were so many great teachers! Now I am an elder and must do some teaching myself, which places the world in a pitiful predicament. My root lama, Thubten Yeshe of Sera Monastery, always told us that we had to become teachers ourselves, but we laughed at the silliness of the idea. However, when one's teachers have died, there is not any other choice.

Many great teachers, Eastern and Western, shared their hearts with me. Among Tibetans I need to thank Lama Thubten Yeshe, Geshe Lhundup Sopa, Geshe Ngawang Dhargyey, Geshe Sonam Rinchen, Lama Thubten Zopa, Khensur Lobsang Tsering, Khenpo Aped, Jhado Rinpoche, Ling Rinpoche, Song Rinpoche, Choden Rinpoche, Serkom Rinpoche, Kalu Rinpoche, the XVIth Gyalwa Karmapa, and especially HH the XIVth Dalai Lama. Among Hindu teachers I must express my gratitude to Swami Gitananda Giri, Swami Venkatesananda, Swami Ranganathananda, Swami Ram Thirta, Pattabhi Jois, and Prof. Satyanarayana Shastry. Amazing, really.

My Western teachers were equally illuminating, and among them I acknowledge professors Harold Garfinkel, Herbert Marcuse, Frederick Olafson, Peter Berger, and W. Russell Ellis. Non-professors included Rabbi Shlomo Carlebach, Saul Alinsky, Ivan Illich, and Willi Unsoeld.

Only four people from these lists survive. When one considers all of them, one can conclude that humanity is doing well and so might be able to afford having me substitute for them. The difference is that most of them managed to tame their minds, while I am struggling. But that is not a poor qualification for a book that is intended to describe such struggles.

Introduction

When a person comes upon two dogs that are about to commence a fight in some street or alleyway, it is natural to attempt to bring the confrontation to a conclusion by shouting at the dogs or chasing them away. Although the human who interferes in these canine affairs has little appreciation of the vital dog-issues that have lent importance to the struggle, it is for certain that the human discounts them and does not consider them so critical that a fight about them is necessary. How do we learn to take the same perspective regarding our own affairs, so that we recognize that most of the conflicts that keep looming before us are unnecessary? Many of the practices of Buddhism are designed to give us that kind of perspective upon our own affairs. Instead of our lending exaggerated importance to whatever it is we are immediately caught up with, one who "practices Buddhism" learns to step back and always read events in the perspective of a broader recognition of what is really important. Such a person can achieve some reconciliation with one's being as one lives daily in one's everyday life. It is not so hard a thing to accomplish that ordinary people cannot have some success at it.

One does not have to meditate but it helps, and of course one of the better known practices of Buddhism is meditation; however, there is a good deal of misunderstanding about it. As a colleague of mine from Sera Monastery, Geshe Thubten Tashi, once explained to me decades ago, one does not meditate so that one can experience "some kind of nice." It is important to meditate so that one can successfully *transform* one's limited perspective in an enduring way, so that we naturally and habitually will act in accord with the dharma most of the time. It is not important to meditate so that one can become accomplished the next time one visits a dharma center, and it is not important to meditate so that one's partner is impressed by one's spiritual growth. It is important to meditate so that we learn to consider our own conflicts as unnecessary as are the conflicts of quarreling dogs, so that it becomes more difficult for us to get angry, and so that we are more able to contribute harmony everywhere we travel, to the benefit of each person we meet. This happens when we keep acting from a place of contentment. That is our primary responsibility, and it is the main reason why we meditate.

I am frequently asked, "What is meditation?" I reply that there are many kinds and many levels of meditation, but that "job-one" is to accept the responsibility for one's own happiness; and if one is unable to do that, at least one should make an effort to develop a capacity to not inflict one's unhappiness or emotional afflictions upon others. Above all, one should not blame anyone for one's unhappiness, since finding a way to be content is exclusively a personal responsibility. At least once each day it is beneficial to check-in with "home," as it were, and reconnect with one's contentment, so that at a minimum one does not keep going around disturbing others like a hungry ghost.

Meditation fosters mindfulness. But meditation is not something to be made a separate occasion; it is an aspect of what we bear continuously. The Tibetan etymology of "meditation" suggests a notion *very* different from what the English term evokes in the minds of most readers. The Tibetan *sgom* (pronounced "góm") literally means "cultivation," "habituation" or "familiarization" more than it means sitting cross-legged on the floor in some sort of mentally induced era of good feelings. "Góm" is the gradual but persistent effort to transform the *habitual* patterns of one's mundane behavior. It is a practice of integrating valued insights into one's psychophysical comportment in a manner that allows them to endure and become a lasting part of our nature. It is because changing our habits requires more than thinking good thoughts that we need to sustain this cultivation over a long period of time. That is why the Gelug founder Tsong Khapa put the *rim* ("gradual," "progressive," "by stages") in Atisha's *lam* ("path"), and this is the centermost insight of Tibetan spiritual culture. In a common dedication prayer that is used to conclude each group or individual meditation session, one expresses one's determination to tame one's mind incrementally, in order to proceed steadily "from one stage to the next stage" ("gong ney gong du"). Tibetans are not believers in any "instant enlightenment" but put their faith in a slow but sure path of gradual self-improvement.

Many traditions have practices of meditation. What distinguishes the Mahayana traditions is that they do not practice simply for the sake of experiencing "some kind of nice" but for the sake of becoming a better human being who can become more capable of bringing peace to others. Therefore, it is less of an absorption exclusively with one's self than are some meditative practices in other traditions.

But this is not a book about meditation; it is a book about *practice* in the mundane world. Mahayana practice involves a commitment to transforming ourselves, and as part of this work we are advised to meditate upon our flaws each day. Especially, we are asked to reflect upon the mistakes we have made in the previous day, to recognize how we could have handled others better and to resolve to improve our behavior in the future. The 19th century Tibetan master Pabongka has written of the Geshe Ban Gungyel, who reviewed his virtuous actions and misdeeds each day, allocating one white pebble to each virtuous actions and one black pebble to each misdeed, allowing him to compare the piles. This book is a bit like this and follows Pabongka's advice (and the advice of Kamalashila before him) to resolve to renounce misbehavior and to cultivate virtues by keeping track, in the way Geshe Ban Gungyel did by reviewing his successes and failures.

Jewish tradition offers the formal requirement of doing this once each year on the Day of Atonement; however, any decent rabbi will teach his congregation that what is done on the Day of Atonement is really a model for what we need to be doing all year long. The special day serves only as a strong reminder of how important is the practice of recalling our faults and developing some resolve to improve our character. In Mahayana Buddhism also, we reflect upon our shortcomings daily in order to transform them. This book is a guide for how to do this kind of analysis of our ordinary affairs.

Each time a disappointment occurs, instead of becoming angry or disappointed, disturbed or depressed, it is best to treat the occasion as a difficult-to-find opportunity to have further practice at maintaining a sense of joy and contentment amidst contrary circumstances; in fact, one can learn to rejoice each time some failure presents another good opportunity for us to study our misdeeds. This book includes many descriptions of failure to act in a Buddhist way in everyday situations. Any time one acknowledges such a failure it is no longer real failure but the first step of practice. Buddhist practice does not mean always acting successfully, but it does mean being frank about assessing how one could act in a more ideal way. These accounts were written in the spirit that Descartes used in his *Discourse on Method*: "I did nothing but wander here and there in the world, trying to be more a spectator than an actor in all the comedies that are played out there; and reflecting particularly in each manner on what might render it suspect and give occasion for erring."

Practice involves analyzing failures skillfully, understanding that they are transitory and open to transformation, and then transforming oneself. This book provides many examples that are models for how this can be done. These models are mundane because our failures and successes are mundane. All of the meaningful solutions are mundane. Our long-term aim is to reduce the frequency with which we become angry toward others and to become more able to bring happiness to each person we meet. Practice can even be making a contest out of how many unhappy, "up-tight" associates one can cheer up in a day. Like the case with the quarreling dogs, fostering harmony is more important than who was right or wrong. That is our responsibility as humans; compassion *is* our humanity. At the very least, we can accept the responsibility to never inflict a sour mood on others. This is where Buddhism can begin.

Some of my friends are cynical about this. They accuse me of being romantic and doubt that the everyday actions of my Tibetan friends differ much from the survival of the fittest practices that are routine in much American life. Such cynicism is prevalent among my colleagues in the university, including some Tibetologists, whose cynicism is so deeply ingrained they may be incapable of accepting that there are people in the world for whom kindness and compassion typically prevail over self-interest. When I report to them the comment by a Sera lama, "I have never hurt any person in this life, and I've never been jealous," they dismiss it as unlikely. They see their own limitations to be universal and project their cynicism and skepticism everywhere. But that is only another form of ignorance, in the way that Tibetans use the word "ignorance": for them, it is not what you do not know that makes you ignorant – it is what you *do* know that makes you ignorant. By projecting the limited world one has understood for oneself onto all our affairs, those affairs are transformed so that they conform to one's way of understanding them. One's mind becomes so filled up with one's prejudices – the matters that are "pre-judged" – that one's mind has no space left for learning what one needs to know most: *what one does not yet know*. Ignorance involves having one's mind so filled with one's own ideas that one is only able to see more of the same, and nothing further. Learning how to undo one's projections and remove them from active operation in order to see more clearly is part of the practice of "emptiness" in Mahayana Buddhism.

A brief story can illustrate that the Tibetans' practice of Buddhism is more than a skill with words and my observations about them more than naïve sentimentalism. The first six months that I lived at Sera, in 1991, I stayed in one of the established "houses" that operate as residential colleges within the larger structure of Sera Jey Monastic University. There were some thirty monks living in my "house," including four teachers, and they all shared a single bathroom. It was not a proper bathroom, since it had no running water (one had to pump the water from a nearby well and carry it in to a large clay container of water in the bathroom). It was really an outhouse, and it served as the sole location for both bathing and defecation for thirty monks. During my six months there, I never once witnessed an argument regarding whose turn it was to use the bathroom. When I returned to my home in Eugene, where I was single parenting my then teenage son Sonam, there was one modern bathroom for two people; and yet several times each week we had an argument over whose turn it was to use the bathroom, and how long that use was taking, etc. Never mind grand theories of ethics or philosophy, and never mind skill in meditation. The proof is in *practice*: the Tibetans sustained no conflict about sharing the sole bathroom. When I once mentioned my discovery to the master of the "house," Geshe Tenpa Chöphal, he said to me, "Well, we eat less than they do in the US." I cannot say whether or not these monks bore any jealousy in their hearts, but I can say that their practice, mundane as it was, served as an inspiration to me.

In the last decade I made a special effort to notice exemplary practices such as this one, and I made many notes about them. Unfortunately, there were also many occasions of failure to practice by myself and by others, and I made notes of them as well, along with some analysis of their main components. These accounts take up the most ordinary of circumstances – answering the door, greeting others, coping with cell phones, driving in heavy traffic, surfing, dealing with misunderstandings, living with attachments, etc. Each story bears a vital message that has its origins in the Kadampa tradition, whose noble early cohort of Tibetan teachers paid special attention to how skillful we are at self-delusion, and how intransigent egoism is despite our best efforts to remove it. It should be easy for the reader to locate him/herself in each account. Again, Buddhist practice does not always involve being successful, but it does require that we examine our actions. To some extent then, this book is that examination, a record of my foolishness if you will, along with accounts of my efforts to address them. It has been an easy book to write, since I have so many failures to choose from. In short, we are learning together.

The stories in this book were written primarily for the sake of getting me to think more about how I could practice better. In doing so, I was able to understand for the first time the true purport of Shantideva's comments on the first page of both his famous *Entering the Path of the Bodhisattva* (*byang chub sems dpa'i spyod pa la 'jugs pa*) and his incredible collection of advice from the Buddha's sutras, *Anthology of Trainings* (*bslab pa kun las btus pa*), which I first studied under Geshe Sonam Rinchen in 1982:

> Here I was not attempting to write for the sake of any others; rather, I have composed these lines only as a means for cultivating a better mind myself, thinking that they will lead me to become more resolved about cultivating virtuous behavior. Even so, if occasionally someone with a similar orientation should see these lines and find them a means for improving their character the composition will have gained added significance. [1]

---

1 The translation here is mine, but a fine contemporary translation has been completed by Charles Goodman and is soon to be released by Oxford University Press.

I

The Peri-pathetic Practitioner

1
How to Answer a Doorbell

The doorbell rang again, this time early in the morning. After months of enthusiastic living, it had not been a good week for me. Not only had I reached the bottom part of the parabolic sine-curve that reflects the inevitable ups-and-downs of daily living, my ordinary relations had not been going well. My extraordinary roommate Kumar, an Ayurvedic masseur whose family in Mysore (where I was living) have been Ayurvedic practitioners for generations, had been giving classes on massage to a dozen Western students at a time, and these students had been spending their days occupying my living room for the previous fortnight. Not only were they spread across the floors of the flat from 10am to 1pm (the timing of the class) they were also practicing massage on themselves or their friends for the rest of the afternoons. I couldn't play music, use the bathroom (which they also dominated, making free use of my precious and hard to obtain US-manufactured toilet paper and shampoos), nor could I conveniently make meals or tea in the kitchen without disturbing the students with noises from the tea-kettle, idli-steamer, or pressure cooker. It was too hot to close the door to my bedroom, which might have afforded me some privacy, as I needed the ventilation to keep from sweating. I felt under siege.

To make matters worse, my roommate had recently taken on a young girlfriend from Germany, who had somehow gotten the idea that my kitchen more properly belonged to her. Or perhaps she had some ideal of communal living that I did not share, and to my surprise I soon found my utensils and supplies being rearranged.

Perhaps I had become too old to be instructed about by a 24 year-old woman. It could also have been that the proximity of this new affair only reminded me about my unhappy new status of being both old and single again. Whichever it was, out of a sense of self-protection I had to let her know that she should not feel any sense of entitlement to my food or cooking supplies and should ask each time before she used anything. This led to some tension between us, the first social tension I had experienced in many months.

The doorbell kept ringing all day with my roommate's clients, who had somehow mistaken me for the butler. Since Kumar was frequently closed inside his room giving a comprehensive massage to a paying customer, it was left to me to answer the door and receive messages, collect the mail, and attend to beggars. Some students, with a greater than usual sense of privilege and entitlement, would want to come inside to wait for Kumar to finish, when it would be left to me to entertain them, provide tea, pens and paper, etc. I had my own work to do, and I began to resent being taken as the Western students' "go-for;" and, naturally, this led to further negative interactions. I resolved not to answer the door any more, even though occasionally it could have been someone who was ringing for me. Some people kept ringing anyway, knowing that I had to be there.

When the door rang early that morning, it was 8 am on the only day of the week that there was no class, and Kumar and his girl-friend had gone away, leaving me at last an opportunity to savor some rare privacy, while also feeling a little depressed and not desiring social interaction. Somehow, I had forgotten about my resolve not to answer doorbells, and I remembered about it only as my hand had already reached for the doorknob. Propelled by the momentum that led my hand to the door, I opened it anyway. Before me there stood a young American women with a closely shaved head and an earring in one ear. I recognized at once that she would require a full orientation to how Kumar organized massage reservations and massage-class registration.

I winced. It was an unmistakable wince. And I spoke, "This is not a good time." The young woman began to declare her inquiry about massage, and I gestured to the book and pen that we had affixed to the door and asked her to leave her questions there. I promised to insure that Kumar would read them, and then I gently closed the door.

Loneliness and personal pain can sometimes render us incapable of generosity. Milarepa used to knock for alms at only the first door of each village, skipping the village altogether if the person there had no food to offer. The Talmud says that one should place a door in each of the four walls of one's house, so that a stranger should not be inconvenienced to walk around the house in order to knock for assistance. But when people feel some emotional depression, they have little capacity for generosity, because these sentiments are usually accompanied by an obsessive preoccupation with one's self.

Some days later I was having breakfast at an Indian neighbor's informal backyard restaurant, and I was speaking with two friends of mine who were interested in the story of how I had discovered Buddhism. I began to regale them with a humorous story about meeting Lama Yeshe in New Zealand in 1975, when this same young woman who had knocked at the door joined our table. We were all in good spirits, and she had a heart that was open sufficiently to let go of any resentment caused by my response to her morning visit to my door, and she participated in the congeniality of the table.

How frequently we hold on to some personal resentment, as if it was a special friend. Most resentment is hardly more than our own imaginings and projections, concretized further by our dwelling on it. We sometimes, or I at any rate, dwell on others' worst qualities, which render their good qualities no space to appear *and develop* – even though the development of other people's good qualities is indeed the principal responsibility that human beings have to each other. This is the "universal responsibility" about which H.H. Dalai Lama often speaks.

This young woman joined Kumar's succeeding massage class, and so we had ample opportunity to interact with each other. After a couple of weeks we had become good friends, solidified in part by some radical political perspectives we shared. She was especially pleased to learn about the 12th century Indian Swami, Basaveswara, who had strongly advocated for gender equality and who has a large number of followers to this day. I had informed her about this unique saint on the occasion of his birthday, which was a public holiday in the Indian State of Karnataka.

After a month had passed, we felt comfortable enough with ourselves to talk about that first encounter. In fact, I broached the topic by offering her an apology. She was surprised to hear it, since she told me that she presumed that I had not recognized her as being the one who was at the door that morning. I replied that I had recognized her all along, and felt shamed by my lack of charity on the occasion. She confessed that on that morning she was feeling extremely insecure and depressed, and that my lack of enthusiasm about her was a blow to her self-esteem at a vulnerable moment, one that only deepened her personal sense of unworthiness. This especially should be noted: quite the opposite of the intimidation that at the time I had projected she was bearing, she herself was feeling vulnerable! How frequently, lacking in charity, we grasp a situation wrongly.

Accordingly, I shared this thought with her: "So let's look carefully at this. You were feeling vulnerable and depressed, projecting all of the power onto me; and I was feeling vulnerable and depressed, projecting all of the power onto you. Yet the very solution to our problems lay in our own hands – to offer loving kindness to each other – although we were impotent about implementing it. Why can most people not experience joy at the approach of another person? Why do our fears keep leading us astray?

Why can we not more frequently be helpers and guides for each other?"

"Well, we finally came to the right position, it just took us a little time," she proposed.

I then pointed out, "But let us correctly identify the moment that was most critical to our success. It was at the breakfast, when you were willing to not harbor any resentment toward me but were able to let it go so easily. If you had held on to it, which is more commonly people's practice, we would still be sources of antagonism to each other!" The observation touched her.

It is important that this be a lesson learned: be *very quick* to surrender one's negative feelings about others. This practical lesson is probably even more important than learning that one should always open one's front door with some generosity of spirit. Nevertheless, opening one's front door with good cheer can become a simple practice that each person can undertake successfully on a daily basis.

2
My Coffee Cup

During my later years my drug of choice has been caffeine, in the form of two cups of coffee each morning. I make a ritual of it every morning, akin to the flower-filled leaf offerings of the Balinese or the ancestor incense-burning of traditional Japanese. It goes like this: turn the stove on; start 18 ounces of water heating; preheat the cup; pulverize four long peppers (*Pipul longum*, an aromatic variety), six coriander seeds and a thumbnail clipping's worth of turmeric root with a mortar and pestle; add one twig of *Ephedra nevadensis* (picked outside my home in Baja California); and boil all together for 3-5 minutes; while it is boiling, I grind enough of the fresh whole beans that I have roasted at home to make two cups; I pour the boiled and seasoned water through a one-cup filter of coffee into my favorite coffee cup, a hand-made mug I have used ever since my divorce, and then I lean back and enjoy paradise. The native North American ephedra imparts a very whole, round flavor to the cup, and contributes to the stimulation of the caffeine in a synergetic way. The spices wake up the taste buds in every part of the tongue, so all the buds are waving gladly as the caffeine hit comes their way: it is a festival of taste. Only when the cup in my hand has become my world's best friend do I sit down to study.

That cup is one of my principal solaces in life. It has large, deep royal blue ceramic inside and out, with the picture of some sea birds glazed on the outside. Its inside communes with my own insides. Surely life's finest pleasures are the simple ones.

Then my former wife came to visit our son and I for two weeks, and while she had a garage sale of some sundries she had been keeping in storage, I left the scene for three days. The morning after I returned I went to make the ritual cup for my morning study, and it was nowhere to be found. I checked all of the cupboards; she had shifted around and re-sorted many of my plates and pots and had added to my collection a few ghosts from our past that she was unable to sell. So I checked the drawers, the sink, the living room, the cupboards a second time, and a third, becoming angrier while my seasoned water boiled away. Did she accidentally sell the cup, I wondered? Or did someone recognize my cup's spiritual powers and secret it away for their own private rituals? I could not believe it—of all our 15 cups, only this one was missing!

I began to rage inside, oh the cherishing of self and the bad karma of a marriage gone sour, striking straight at the heart of me once again! But who contributes the energy to this, I reflected? None but my *own* grasping desire, and attachment, fuels the damage doing. How can I, who during my morning meditative practice ritually gives away "all my worldly possessions for the sake of all mother sentient beings," become so unraveled by *one* single coffee cup? Recognizing that the time for the "real" spiritual work had again arrived, I headed into my bedroom to my meditation table and sat down to meditate on the origins of my anger, in order to try to eliminate it. One must work hard and with perseverance if one is to reduce the afflictive emotions.

No sooner had my buttocks hit the seat, in fact it was a split second before I landed, that I saw my cup. There it was, sitting on my meditation table, filled with some loose Tibetan incense that my former wife had left over from one of her boxes and which she was donating to my meditations. Aha! The spiritual power of my caffeine cup was indeed recognized by her. She had even placed the cup in a suitable spiritual environment. I laughed out loud. Oh, the teaching—how quickly we hand over our souls to the pettiest of the attachments that bind us to the tedious suffering that only *we ourselves* fashion. No wonder this work I have taken on requires three countless aeons.

3
One Way Not to Meditate

I am fortunate to live in a beautiful location in Baja California Norte, about 200 miles south of the Tijuana/ San Ysidro international border crossing. My house, which is built out of local stones that washed down along the adjacent arroyo (dry creekbed), is nestled in a sand dune that overlooks the Pacific Ocean, and each morning I rise at first light and climb the dune to a south-facing promontory that has a 270° open sweep of the sky, ocean and hills. In the east, the mountains in the distance rise to 10,000 ft., and I have even stood atop that peak to gaze back at these dunes. I have a little meditation nest at the promontory, and when the sun shows its first glints between a couple of the near-most hills it usually finds me reciting my daily *Ganden Lha Gye-ma*, the praise to Lama Tsong Khapa and the Buddha-field.

Long ago I made a promise to a teacher, Song Rinpoche, to recite once each day this fabulous praise that condenses all of the essential teachings of Buddhism. My commitment was the price I was made to pay for a full week of instruction from Song Rinpoche (who was then about 80 years of age) on the extensive Lama Chöpa ritual, which is an expanded version of the daily *Ganden Lha Gye-ma* recitation. Song Rinpoche offered the most phantasmagorically detailed description of the Tibetan tantrika imaginary universe that I have ever received, and that includes the many splendid teachings I have received from H.H. Dalai Lama, the XVIth Gyalwa Karmapa, H.H. Sakya Trinzen, Dilgo Khyentse, Ling Rinpoche, Chagdud Rinpoche, and many other masters. Song Rinpoche sat explaining the details of the Lama Tsong Khapa merit field visualization for many hours at a time, motionless with his long white Colonel Sanders goatee, calm while intense, as the rest of us prayed for the quick arrival of a brief recess that would permit us to go and urinate – a recess that on some days never came. Song Rinpoche provided so vivid a description of the tutelary merit field that after the teaching I easily fell into a regular morning practice of *Ganden Lha Gye-ma*, which I have continued now for four decades.

Here at my home where the Baja desert meets the sea, it is even easier to do this practice. I just climb up the dune, 120 steps that take less than two minutes, and enter the ambience of this seat of my contentment. And the location has the additional advantage of allowing me to view the day's swell, so by the end of my short session I have not only praised all of the buddhas, I also know whether or not I will surf that day, and which of my several surfboards I will use. Subliminally – more through my skin than by way of my mind – I also absorb the pace of the day's rhythmic cycling of wave-sets. That my meditation is thus rendered pitiful I will readily admit, but it is still fulfilling and offers a sense of benevolence, and that is at least part of the point of a meditation session.

On this particular morning I arose and climbed the dune. As usual, there was no one else at this moment of dawn except two Mexican fishermen who were launching their craft down at the beach, far below me. I happily recited the praises. The horizon was clear as the sun rose, and the ocean was calm. The waves were lapping from a glassy ocean as if inviting me to join. Soon I came to the section of my prayer where I offer all of my belongings and aspirations to others, so that these others may use them for the sake of their own spiritual expansion. The idea is each day to formally practice a little letting-go of what one likes to hold to obsessively; it is a sort of simulation of the generosity that needs to accomplish one day, as soon as one has one's act together. You should have seen me – the relinquishing was visible in my hands, my whole body was a mudra. I have so well cultivated the mere form of renunciation that I can look devout even while I am really studying waves.

And then something unexpected happened. A large camper-van rolled up with about eight surfboards piled up on top, and five young US surfers – who were returning from a long surfari in southern Baja – spilled out, and in a matter of four minutes they had unfurled their board bags, waxed the boards, suited up, and were heading out across to *my* beach, to surf *my* waves before I even got there.

What a total phony I am! Here in the midst of a meditative absorption, cultivating only the highest aspirations prior to my surf session – I had just finished dedicating everything I possessed for the benefit of others – when a few of these imagined "others" had the audacity to turn up in the flesh. I was upset, since I now would be forced to share my surf session with some agro-competitive surfers nearly 40 years younger than me. Worse still, they would surely be capable of out-surfing me, leaving this old fellow with just some leftovers. How did they not recognize that this was *my* parade?

Many years ago, perhaps in the late 1970's, when I had come to know Lama Yeshe well and Lama had come to know me, he concluded wistfully, "You know, I think maybe you take refuge in beach!" Yes, the beach *has* been a longstanding place of refuge for me; but at the end of his life, Lama Yeshe also seemed to take refuge in his own beach that he found in northern California not far north of Pacific Grove, where Lama chose to spend his final year. I have found a perfect beach here in Mexico that is like living in a permanent retreat. As Lama used to say, we need to cultivate "an affluence of satisfaction," and here is a place where I can effectively accomplish this important work of life. Once, when I told a girlfriend in Oregon that I was migrating to Baja California, she scolded me, "I cannot believe that you of all people would be retreating from society and abandoning your social responsibilities!" I replied, "This is no retreat. This is a wholesale surrender."

In any event it has worked out quite well – the silence here runs rich enough for me to suck from like it was mother's milk itself, and it seeps into my marrow. The single difficulty is that I had no choice but to bring my own miserable self here along with me, which keeps throwing wrenches into the satisfaction thing: there I was at the top of *my* dune, looking over *my* beach, when some strangers roll in like they owned my waves too! I was unable to tamp down my self-grasping.

The key to practice is to rejoice whenever a fresh opportunity to learn one's weaknesses appears.

In meditation it is important to remember that the point is not to be Buddha – it may take three countless aeons to realize that you are *already* Buddha. The point is to *observe* your root flaws. Until you can at least notice them, the Herculean task you have taken on cannot even commence, and such ignorance can hurl itself into endless cycles without any chance of slowing itself. So there I had my dharma task– it was to make my ugly, selfish self the one-pointed focus for my meditative abiding. There was no avoiding it.

What can be so downright difficult about sharing waves?! Sure, I'm old, and because of my three heart surgeries and two pacemaker implants I can barely paddle strongly enough to remain competitive; but aren't there waves aplenty? I mean, they do keep coming wave-after-wave, don't they? So I could certainly open my heart enough to share them with a mere five live (and not abstract) sentient beings. It is one's *own* attitude that creates the dissatisfaction. But the selfishness in one's stomach is not so easy to relinquish – the "me," "mine," and all that. It is so much fun playing in the surf by oneself! But why not be generous to these kids? And how many thousands of surfers will show up here after them as the years roll on – should I not feel glee at the prospect of anticipating so many new opportunities to teach myself how to become more generous? All I need to do is overcome my fervent attachment to hoarding every one of the ocean's waves for myself.

It is easy to let go when there is nothing at stake. It only counts as "practice" when one works steadily at letting-go those things one's stomach has seized upon firmly with undiluted determination. But this time it was too much for me. I descended the dune in defeat, but I still had twenty minutes to work on it before I paddled out to join these usurpers.

4
My Knee's Teaching

Most Western students of Tibetan Buddhism eventually confront an interior limit to their study of dharma: their knees. Accustomed to sitting in chairs, when they are forced to sit cross-legged on the floor for many hours at a sitting, their pain can render them deaf to truth itself. My life-long yoga teacher Dr. Swami Gitananada of Pondicherry used to say, "The typical Westerner is crucified on the cross of the chair," and he explained that chair-sitting leads to a host of physical maladies. I used to joke in Tibetan with my main teacher at Sera Jey Monastic University, the Khenpo Lobsang Tsering, by saying that while I may have been unable to follow each one of the subtle points from his brilliant and patient two hour-long exegeses of text, at least my knees were becoming enlightened. This was usually just before I would stumble out of his room, careening off one of the walls.

In fact, I was able to sit in the lotus position better than most Westerners. This was because I spent years backpacking and camping, logging many thousands of miles in the high country, which requires preparing one's meal about a fire while sitting in the cross-legged position. After that, I lived with Aboriginal people in central Australia for two years, and their default position, again around a fire, was to sit cross-legged. I remember that they would scold me if during any sacred ceremonies my back would droop or I would lean on an elbow for a moment: only a straight back was acceptable! So by the time I came to Nepal and India and sat for long discourses on dharma by Tibetan masters, my legs were quite well prepared for the challenge. The Tibetans incorrectly read that as my having accomplished a great deal of meditation. Because Tibetans are so accustomed to undertaking long and serious meditative retreats, they tend to overestimate Westerners' capacities in this regard.

Sometimes it is the case among Buddhist meditative practitioners that the quality of one's meditative practice is gauged from how comfortable, and for how long, one is able to sit in a lotus or half-lotus position. This, of course, is foolish, but humans are fools if they are anything. My fellow Westerners would struggle hard to cope with sitting cross-legged, and after an hour of teaching it became evident which ones were the long-time students and practitioners and which ones were the newcomers. My knees always lied on my behalf, and I was able to outlast most in a room, not because I had completed long meditative retreats, which was the case for some, but simply because of a life of living outdoors in the wilderness and with Aboriginal people.

I sometimes enjoyed the effect, especially when a small segment of the robed Western *sangha* (monks and nuns) would flaunt the sanctity of their practice. It was fun to watch the lowering of the self-esteem of some who considered their practice superior to laypersons like me – and other Westerners who mostly held my Western academic interests in low regard – when they were forced to lift up their knees for a rest, while I went on sitting comfortably. While I have dragged my knees through a few long meditative retreats, I certainly have invested more knee-time in listening to dharma teachings by great masters than I have invested in meditative practice.

The year that Sera Jey in South India completed its large new meditation/prayer/teaching hall, His Holiness the 14th Dalai Lama came to inaugurate it. Since he was to give a full week of instruction on Khedrup Je's fabulous *Encyclopedia on Emptiness* (*sTong mthun chen mo*), a critical and lengthy text in the Gelug tradition, I made the trip for the teachings along with a hundred other Westerners. The teachings were extraordinary, and I was able to follow the text each step of the way as the Dalai Lama gave his explanation of each passage. I could not help but notice that many of the great Western meditators, both robed and unrobed, kept losing their place in the text, whereas I was always able to keep up, or if His Holiness skipped across some section (which was rare) I could quickly locate where he picked up. Not only that, after several days of teaching that lasted all day I noted that many of these Western practitioners were no longer able to remain cross-legged and were beginning to keep lifting their knees up for relief, while I was experiencing no knee pains. Thinking this way, my ego kept getting puffed up higher and higher, and all the while I noticed that about me there was new-found respect for this "intellectual" (i.e. me). It was a total ego-trip, and I was basking in it.

One afternoon, perhaps it was the fifth day of the teaching, His Holiness the Dalai Lama went on longer than usual. It is possible that he was attempting to finish the long text before the end of the week that had been scheduled for it. The audience was exhausted, many were napping (the percentage of napping Tibetans exceeded the percentage of napping Westerners, but universally it had become a soporific hall), and I myself had fallen into an elaborate daydream. Either the Dalai Lama had become aware of the lateness of the hour or he observed that he had lost his audience, but he stopped his teaching very suddenly, and without the usual long closing prayer rose to leave.

I had been sitting in the full lotus position for about two hours, and both legs had fallen completely asleep. Lost in my day-dream, I did not notice the precise moment when His Holiness ended his exegesis and became aware that the afternoon teachings had concluded only when everyone in the hall began to stand up for the recession of the Dalai Lama. It would not do for me to remain sitting while His Holiness was standing, so I leapt up, and in one go went from the full lotus to standing. The ligaments in my left knee must have been fully stretched and relaxed, and when my leg muscles contributed the added strain to them, one of my ligaments snapped. I badly injured my left knee.

My knee was in pain for the final two days of teachings – no more lotus position for me – and the knee swelled up badly. I figured that it would take me some weeks to get over it. But I did not realize at the time that it would be permanent, or at least as permanent as I am, and chronic enough to cause my left thighbone to slip out of the knee socket many hundreds of times a day, each and every day. Day after day, until the end of my life. It doesn't take much for me to get it back into place, which I must do any time I try to climb or descend stairs, run, carry a pack, etc. As I write this at my desk, I am even now having to stand up and 'click' my knee back into its socket, something I do all day long, every day. By the time I reached 60 years of age, I grew sick of it, and I have come to be relieved to consider that due to my inevitable death I will not be forced to go on readjusting it until the end of time.

Whenever I hear this click, which resonates loudly as I set the knee back into its socket (there it is again, just a minute ...), it says to me: "Mind your ego, Ken; it was your ego-grasping that got you into this mess." I am reminded of my Lama, Thubten Yeshe, who upon climbing the teaching throne always would stand, raise his right hand and snap his thumb and fore-finger together before sitting down, as a reminder to himself that life is very impermanent and that it is destined to end in an instant. Recalling this is helpful for reducing one's pride. My knee is an even better reminder than a finger snap, and not only because it is louder – it bears the karma of my own flaw in character. It mocks my every attempt to sit and pretend I am a real practitioner. Now most of the *sangha*, whose egoism was probably less than mine all along, can sit in the dharma teachings longer than I can. Each opportunity to eat humble pie should be cherished.

5
Everybody's Ignorance

Our daily lives is a comedy of errors. When ordinary conflict occurs, we inspect the situation to determine who is at fault, ourselves or the other person. Normally we convince ourselves that the other person is the root of the problem; however, the truth is that more frequently *both* persons are at fault even as each blames the other. The result is that no one will be able to make any progress. We adorn our practice with sweet prayers and lofty words, but when it comes to treating our neighbors with generosity we find that we are unable to give generously, except as a show. If only we could remember that it is not always the case that one person is right and the other wrong: *both* persons may have flaws. The current Israeli-Palestinian conflict is another case in point.

During one course of dharma teachings I had become very absorbed with a Tibetan text that explains many subtle aspects of Middle Way analyses of faulty thinking. Each day during the afternoon, our lama would permit us to pose some "questions" about emptiness. It is important for a teacher to hear students' questions because that way the teacher can better come to know what the students have understood; without occasionally connecting with the minds of the students, it is difficult to communicative effectively; however, too frequently these questions become a forum for a display of students' egos. Questions become long and intricate, little more than advertisements for the questioner. Questions can be a tangle of confusions as students try to sort out and display what they know. One course of teachings featured a dharma student who never let a question-time pass without posing some long and foggy question. She also had the habit of starting her question with some very quick speech that was highly effective for securing the floor, but then slowing down her speech to a slow crawl as soon as she had captured everyone's attention; sometimes it could require several minutes for her to finish her question, using up much of the question period, and the longer her question (and the more English words used) the less was the sense the lama would be able to make of it. This would result in her having to repeat the question, which worked in her favor and required even more time.

This became a daily occurrence, to the point that a couple of the senior students could be seen to wince visibly each time this student was called upon for her question. We are easily influenced when several people share a response, so when these senior students observed each other's wincing, their negative assessment was confirmed, which made their feelings only heavier, to the point of incapacitating their ability to recognize any intelligent aspect the questioning might have had. This is common: when a course of one's ignorance is confirmed by others, it becomes hardened, making the discovery of one's own errors more difficult.

I joined the wincers, and this was not lost upon the student questioner, who began to dislike me for my dislike of her, not an uncommon variety of misunderstanding in mundane affairs, if a bit circular. I appeared arrogant to the student, for the reason that I was arrogant. It has been said by Gyaltsab Je that a person who has good moral practices but who does not understand emptiness is not to be faulted; however, a person who becomes conceited about his or her understanding of emptiness is to be condemned by all. Well, we wincers were the latter sort. Of course we would prefer to defend ourselves by emphasizing that we could better understand emptiness by sticking to the text and not being distracted by extraneous questions that were more self-centered than text-centered. So here we have another one of these cases of two wrongs that interfere with each other, and the student-questioner and I handled the situation mostly by avoiding each other. We were two pathetic practitioners of dharma.

One day, before the teachings began, the habitual questioner came up to where I was sitting to ask me a question. It was something like "Do you have the *prasad*?" "*Prasad*" means "offering" in Sanskrit, but I didn't know what she was talking about. I asked her what she meant, and she repeated her question. Quick to become impatient, in part because it is my nature and in part because I was predisposed to become impatient with this person in particular, I replied that as far as I knew *prasad* meant offering (I gestured to the temple shrine's offering bowls), and that I didn't know what she was talking about. She exclaimed, "I know that! Oh... just forget about it!" and then stormed off. I really was willing to answer her question, but I was not able to elicit its meaning or its purpose. I am sure that she knew what she meant, but she also presumed that I must also know what she meant; her conclusion was that I was only trying to be difficult with her because I disliked her, a wrong presumption that lacked skill on her part. I had no idea what it was that she was asking.

The presumption that a person one is addressing understands something said just in the way one understands it oneself is a projection that usually has little basis in fact. One thing I learned from 30 years of university teaching is that if I can count on anything, I can count on my students not understanding most of what I say in the way that I intended it. When I was a newly minted teacher, I presumed just the opposite, i.e. that most of the students did understand what I was saying. The act of believing in the independent truth and facticity of the meanings that one projects upon experience is the very definition of "ignorance." She was convinced that the meaning of her question was apparent on its face, and so she incorrectly concluded that I was deliberately giving her a hard time. Neither was true.

This is a suitable illustration of when one must take action – not necessarily to make friends of the other, but to remove from one's heart the negative feelings one may have for another person that have grown to the point of disturbing relations, a disturbance that make dharma practice difficult. Again, the problem is with oneself. Accordingly, a very good dharma practice is to identify the person one genuinely dislikes and transform one's feelings about the person. One should heed the advice to make effort to see all persons as attractive! It may be hard to do, but I always recall Lama Yeshe's most often tendered advice: "You *can* do!"

It is easy to develop positive feelings for someone that one does like, so that offers us little opportunity for learning how to develop kindness. On the other hand, a person one dislikes is a fabulous candidate for facilitating one's evolution. One can place *that* person in front of one during one's meditation and sit with that person until one's habitual feelings about that person improve. This can be made a daily part of one's meditative practice (remember, "meditation" in Tibetan is really the word for "habituation"). The point here is to re-habituate oneself to more positive sentiments towards a person. It is a long and slow process, so it is good to try to speed this evolution by choosing as recipients for one's kindness people one does not like. First you try it alone, when the other person is not there to annoy you; only later do you risk putting it into practice. If one succeeds in purifying one's own contaminated mind-stream, it usually will be enough, and somehow the everyday affairs will set themselves right quickly! This itself is proof that one has indeed had a hand in contaminating the flawed relations. How often has one heard the statement, "Oh, he's not so bad after all," as if that "he" was the *sole* source of any of the change, denying the role played by the transformation of one's own attitude.

One day at lunch I got up from my seat at the cafeteria table to get something to drink. When I returned, I noticed that the aforementioned student-questioner had taken the seat next to me. I instantly accepted that as an opportunity to improve our relations. When I returned, and she saw that I was the person sitting next to her, she got up and took her tray over to another table. I commented to her, "You don't have to do that." One of the most important dharma practices, one that is repeated endlessly in Buddhist teachings, is that one should treat people *impartiality*. All of the small differences that distract and preoccupy us really amount to nothing. Especially, we should treat others without favoritism and be generous in spirit toward those with whom we may disagree. While we generally wish to eat lunch next to friends, no students of the dharma should be *unwilling* to sit next to other dharma seekers. Surely they, more than others (one would hope), would have some capacity to overcome their desires and aversions and be tolerant.

The incident caused both of us to reflect. I offered an account of what happened to a mutual friend of ours, and I simultaneously began to take inventory of what I had done to contribute to such a state of affairs. Our friend generously discussed the situation with the student-questioner, and by the time the weekend was over, the student-questioner had realized that matters had gone too far. She arrived at the teachings on Monday morning with a kind gift for me of the very best quality Darjeeling tea, the sort of gift that one would give a lama. I recognized the resolution of our dilemma at once, and kissed her on the cheek, thanking her. In a finger-snap our difficulties were resolved, and resolved for good. On this occasion at least, good will overcame bad will. The next time I met her, a few years later, she had become a Buddhist nun.

The secret is to learn how to *multiply* such occasions in one's everyday life. The bad news is also the good news that there is no shortage of opportunities for overcoming hostility with kindness! The practice can be augmented further by learning to rejoice each time one has been treated badly, since it offers one more opportunity to practice being kind; that is, one celebrates that another opportunity has presented itself for purifying one's mind-stream of one's own negative feelings. It *can* be done!

6
The Sand Path in the Dune

My home is nestled one-third of the way up the leeward side of a 200-foot coastal sand dune in Baja California. There is a path that leads from my stone steps to a long-standing track that climbs steeply to the dune's crest. Each morning, within a minute or two of arising I throw on my old tennis shoes and climb up to the top of the dune to meditate. I like to rise between first light and the moment when the sun breaches the horizon in the east, so that I can catch its first rays as I reach the crest of the dune. What is remarkable about this dune is that it runs for half a dozen miles to end steeply just eighty yards south of my house. During my morning meditation I have a vista below me: in the west, the waves are peeling across the point in a windless, still ocean, dolphins are scavenging for fish in a rhythmic swimming that resembles the moving ponies of a merry-go-round, and pelicans are diving sharply for their breakfasts; cranes bathe in the lagoon; fifty miles in the east there is a 10,000-foot peak of granite that is sharply spotlighted by the first lances of winter sun rising in the south; and in the south is a vast desert plain where in the distance the eight hundred mile stretch of the California coastal chaparral botanical regime finally gives way to cactus.

Most of the winter I am the only person to climb the dunes. As a rule, Mexicans do not go in for recreational climbing, and many of them are too overweight from a diet heavy in fats and sodas to handle the steep sandy slope easily. My other neighbors are mostly elderly retirees from Southern California, and they do not visit the top of the dunes from one year to the next. I have learned that if I step up the dune in an orderly way my footprint's impression will endure to the succeeding day, and I can create some very neat steps that will halve the difficulty of my climb. It is like hiking in snow, where those who follow the leaders have a much easier time of it than the leader does, simply by stepping in the other person's footprints. I especially enjoy the rare rainstorm, after which I am able to cut some especially clean footsteps into the dune, steps that can endure a week or more.

In the summer and during vacation times (spring break, Xmas break, Memorial and Labor Day weekends, when the Bàja beaches are the site for many beach parties) there are a few other climbers who visit the crest for the view. Most of them seem to have two left feet, which obliterates the neat steps I have labored to preserve. The kids have a blast but are naturally inclined to turn the foot track into a slide zone, making my climb the next morning a considerable workout. There is an occasional out-of-condition adult who tries the climb. Such persons may need to pause to catch their breath after every couple of steps; eventually, usually just below the top, they need to rest and lie down in the sandy swale, where they can resemble a beached walrus. A few climbers are so unused to exertion that they need to branch off into the surrounding vegetation to get enough purchase on the soil to be able to keep stepping. In this fashion they needlessly destroy vegetation and unnecessarily widen the track up the dune. I once speculated that one of the climbers who preceded me must have been an elephant.

As the reader may be able to tell, I am well and truly *attached* to my early morning sand path. Now, if one wishes to become attached to something, I would recommend that one find something that is naturally a bit more enduring than a foot-track in a sand dune. Surely nothing is permanent, but in the way of the world, a sand path is to be rated at the low end of durability. Why do small children cry when the tide washes away their precarious sand castle? Because they have reified the castle, i.e. turned it into an independent thing seemingly permanent despite its tenuous existence. What foolishness it is to feel pride at perfecting a righteously tidy track that allows me to sprint up to the top in the morning without having to increase the rate at which I breathe. Why does attachment grow *spontaneously* whenever there is the slightest satisfaction with a state of affairs? Can we really prevent ourselves from becoming attached to anything and everything? How does one celebrate life without becoming attached to things?

There is a long-standing teaching in both Buddhist dharma and Hindu spiritual instruction, and that is to develop *equanimity*. Accordingly, the advice here is to never become displeased with any state of affairs, nor become elated about any situation, but to treat all experiences equally, as if everything tasted just the same. The Buddhists tell an allegory that if you give a cup of water to a god or a sage, it will think it tastes like nectar, but if you give the same cup of water to a hungry ghost, it will taste like pus to them. An ordinary person will think it tastes like water; hence, our experience depends upon the mind that we bring to the experience. The advice is to transcend the experience by not being influenced by it in a positive way (which will lead to attachment) or a negative way (which will lead to disappointment or anger).

When people hear this metaphor, they pay the most attention to the advice against becoming upset when something goes wrong. And that is an important piece of advice to consider. Accordingly, when due to the right combination of attention, rainfall, lack of wind, and the simple care of daily cultivation, I have sculpted one fine set of "steps" up the dune, and someone comes by and wrecks the entire path ("Can't they see before their eyes?" "Which idiot is it who sneaked onto my property unseen last night?"). The opportunity here is to *not* be influenced even a bit; accommodate oneself to the way of the world. Rather than generating self-righteous anger that will only harm one's heart, reduce the function of one's immune system and lead to further unhappiness, there is an alternative: just let-go of all that. Step on, and move forward to the morning meditation with benevolence in one's heart. That benevolence is a healing force and is in the point of meditation in the first place.

But this is only half of the practice. The real route to not becoming upset is to not have overdone the taking of pleasure part in the first place. Yes, make the steps in the sand. Yes, utilize them. Yes, feel some oneness with one's habitat, a sense of belonging to it, as if a real symbiosis is in play. But don't try to possess it. Don't convert it to any idea of "my dune" or "my path," and don't "conquer" anything. Realize that its being is a quickly transiting interconnectedly dependent being, a "*ten drel*" (literally, "dependent arising"). *Ten drel* meditation is one of the best kinds of meditation. It will convince you that the sand is not going to do anything other than be blown away. Just live, without trying to freeze every good part into some permanence that one can possess.

The poet William Blake has written:

> He who binds to himself a joy
> Does the winged life destroy.
> But he who kisses the joy as it flies
> Lives in eternity's sunrise.

The heart of the teaching here is that ownership is fools' play. Of course the practice is more difficult than simply reading the words.

Just how does one enjoy something without beginning to grasp for it? How does one experience pleasure without having the urge to perpetuate the experience and strengthen the drive that develops (like laboratory rats) to the point of a single-minded obsession? That is, how do we free ourselves from our own minds! How can we *use* those minds to assist us in severing a few of the links of the chain that enslaves us, a chain fabricated by our habitual patterns of behaving? Put in the most pertinent terms, just how can I make a convenient sand path and enjoy it, without having it become the cause of more unhappiness?

7
Anger Makes You Ugly

A common Tibetan saying has it that "A person's beauty is ruined by being short-tempered." I have lived the truth of this aphorism. The texts of Buddhism are rich with accounts of the many shortcomings of anger. In his *Compendium of Advice*, Shantideva cautions people against becoming angry too frequently, since the grimacing, the clenching of one's teeth, the furrowing of one's brow, and associated scowling – when repeated too often – after some years will result in very ugly and displeasing lines appearing as *permanent* parts of one's visage. Shantideva suggests that once one's face has developed these lines of anger, they are impossible to remove, and they will render it more difficult to attract people's good humor. The point is that once these scowling muscles become well developed, the karma of an angry temperament will be carried in an obvious and visible way by one's physiognomy, especially one's face, and one may begin to look like a wrathful being. The advice here may be reduced to a slogan: "Abolish anger so you don't grow ugly."

Other Buddhist texts warn that one instant of becoming angry is capable of destroying all the merit one may have amassed during a thousand eons of virtuous behavior. Further, the system of the six perfections of bodhisattvas (saints whose love and compassion are limitless – bodhisattvas display a superior form of loving kindness) includes as the third perfection the perfection of Patience. The first time I read Shantideva's chapter on "Patience" many decades ago from his *Entering the Path of a Bodhisattva*, I wept. I was moved not only because becoming angry too easily has been the most abiding flaw in my own character, but also because *despite* the fact that Shantideva had written so clearly and comprehensively a thousand years ago, it has had almost no effect upon humankind's capacity to overcome its shortcomings! This caused me to consider very seriously the possibility that there may really be little hope for the human race, whereupon I cried.

Not only has Shantideva's magnificent account had little effect upon humanity, years later I was to discover that his account was to have little effect upon *my own* ability to reduce my propensity to become angry. Shantideva's writings were hardly more than some nice words that I appreciated, like so much of the dharma reading I do, and I was incapable of cultivating a strong enough meditative self-pacification to draw my cerebral appreciation down into the viscera of my body's habitual energy flows to make any real change. In the end, this failure (even over the decade subsequent to my discovering Shantideva's teaching) contributed to the failure of my marriage. Naturally, this in turn led to more grimacing, a lot of it, including two years of constant brow-furrowing following our divorce, furrowing that is now etched permanently into my forehead, warning others away before I have even opened my mouth. It has left me with just the visage Shantideva described, and which I read about before I had developed the furrows!

The shortcomings of anger, however, exceed even these difficulties. The texts also refer to a greater danger ... that one's anger has the power to stir up the afflicted emotions *of others*, thereby setting into motion a chain of ill-will and misbehavior that is difficult to stop and that in the end pollutes the mental continua of a large number of people, in serial fashion.

Harming others is the cardinal misdeed of a Buddhist practitioner. One should try to cultivate a real concern for the welfare of others. What is easier is to bear a concern for the welfare of one's own child, since one's child is the very last person on earth one wishes to pollute with a poor habit of becoming angry. So the recommendation is that one should commence a practice of patience by beginning with people dear to one.

After my son returned to Eugene following his college graduation, I had an opportunity to overcome anger. Since his east coast college had ended several weeks before our term in Oregon, his arrival coincided with the final two weeks of our academic year. As a college professor, I always found the last weeks of the year to be the most difficult weeks. One feels rushed to finish the course curriculum in an adequate way, and then one must test and grade one's students at a time when nearly all of them are exhausted, stressed, concerned about their graduation, and practically merciless in their eagerness to place the pressures of modern grade inflation upon their professors. Since I had taken the Memorial Day weekend off to attend my son's graduation at Swarthmore, I had fallen behind in my grading papers. Moreover, I needed to pack up and move out of my rented apartment close to campus and prepare to spend the summer in Deer Park, Wisconsin. It was at this time that my son decided to visit – not so much to visit me, but to visit his best friends from high school, some of whom were graduating from the university at which I teach and were my students.

As soon as the sweet boy arrived, with my students' papers spread about the living room floor, he became ill with a high fever, sore throat, and chills. The house was ceded over to him. I carried my papers to my bedroom and then raced around completing a thousand and one last minute details. After two weeks of this, I had become fully stressed. My final job was packing my Eugene belongings into my personal storage unit, which required many trips back-and-forth from my apartment to the storage unit. Finally, on the morning of the expiration day for my lease, I carried the last load (with my son's help) and heaved a great sigh of relief. As I drank some lemonade, even though I was late for an appointment with a student in my office, I spied one more vital possession that had to be transported to the storage unit: the vacuum cleaner, which had been left behind for the cleaning up. I shrieked. I cussed and fumed and totally lost it right in front of my son. It was the culmination of two weeks of abundant stress and little sleep. It even felt good to let loose that way, I am ashamed to say, and so I gave myself over to it. It was a shameless display, although since it was an anger that was directed to no one, it may not have been one of those angers that would destroy the merit of a thousand aeons. But it would prove destructive, as I will explain.

My son, bless his heart, told me to get a grip on myself. Genuinely frightened by the rage of his father in the primordial way that most children are, he instructed that there was no need for such a display, and that in any event the outburst served no constructive purpose. He observed that the end was near, and that one more trip to the storage unit was a very small matter, considering how many trips had already been made. I had been simply grasping the notion that "The job is done."

Of course he was right. He caused me to recall the advice that it is not right to become angry over trivial things since that can have long-term negative consequences that will outlive the pertinence of the trivial matters. And I even felt some joy that my son held such solid wisdom. But I didn't really feel bad, since I conveniently excused it as part of my nature. I consoled myself with the delusion that perhaps it was good to expel the energy. Following the outburst, I continued with the last day's endless chores, and that evening we finally got off on our cross-country journey. As we drove along the Columbia River to eastern Oregon on our way to Boulder, Colorado, I finally had time to reflect upon the shortcomings of my anger.

After that I thought nothing more of it. The next day we drove through Idaho and northern Utah through featureless country, an ideal landscape for recovery, and on the following day (sleeping well each night) we drove through Wyoming into Colorado. Once in Boulder, I dropped my son off at his mother's condominium (she herself was in Tibet) and spent an additional day there recovering from the driving. But my son's mood changed. Now that *he* had the responsibility to fix a temporary home for himself and to face the work of finding his first post-college job, so that he could support himself (as he was eager to do, bless him), he was the one to become tense while I began to feel relaxed and relieved of responsibilities. Under these reversed circumstances the one thing he was not interested in was in last-minute advice from his father – not about cooking, not about exercise, and not about job-hunting.

The second of the two evenings, I offered him the last counsel I would have the opportunity to give him before his adulthood commenced, and I offered it with both love and charity in my heart. I included in the counsel some advice about car care, and he revealed to me that he still did not feel confident as a driver in urban conditions. He also informed me that the first thing he was going to do with my old car that I had given him was to cover up the "Cherish Others" bumper sticker. As he put it, "I'm going to find any bumper sticker I can to cover that up so people don't think I'm a faggot." He was perhaps correct that making a show of one's moral superiority was a sort of flag-waving that in no way ensures that any good deeds will occur; nevertheless, the conversation deteriorated from there.

After some more unsolicited final advice, he had reached his limit, and his body started to tremble the same way that my body had done several days earlier. Look at what I had taught him! He could take no more, and his anger exploded in my face. Naturally, he laid the blame for his anger upon me. And he was right, although not for the reason that he thought. I was not wrong about his needing to learn how to cook, nor about his wearing a helmet when he rides a bike, nor about continuing to read good books. I was wrong in that I had succeeded in providing him with a vivid model for how to become uncontrollably angry.

Such models are especially forceful, and are deeply rooted, when they channel some of the life force from a father to a son. They operate at such a deep level of energy patterning and behavior transfer that there is no way to uproot them with mere words or counsel. When asked how one teaches a child not to get angry, the Dalai Lama once replied that words will not be effective and that the only recourse was to teach by example, by not getting angry.

So I had blown it in the worst possible way: I had managed to teach my son how to become angry. What a sorry fruit my affliction has led to. My own flawed character came to pollute the mind stream of the son that I so cherished and admired. Moreover, the deed was a *fait accompli*. It cannot be undone! It had already found its place in his mental continuum, unknown perhaps even to him, and was ready to be made available whenever he proved incapable of controlling himself. This is the real shortcoming of anger: it harms the people we care about by turning them into people who perpetuate the affliction, once they have internalized this manner of being. And in this instance, my behavior – during the previous week, and over decades – was the direct cause. In this regard, the question that naturally arises here is that if I am such a failure in this practice, what qualifications do I have for writing this book?

The resolution to become more responsible for each other must be actual, not theoretical. And upon considerable reflection, I have begun to put some conclusions into practice. The resolution to defeat anger needs to take shape in the most tangible ways possible. Since anger is something that is tactile, that we feel as a growing heat in one's stomach, there is a natural object present for us to focus upon. This growing heat flares with tremendous rapidity, but since it feeds on the situation's particulars all that we need to do is to shift our attention *away* from those particulars and *to* that flaring heat itself. Recognize that that heat, right there, is the real enemy. Since it is easy to identify, the practice can proceed each time straightaway. A swift defeat of the anger can be achieved by disassociating it from any of the particulars that are feeding it, and one tames it by denying it that fuel. Make its taming into your *sadhana* (disciplined regular practice), and stay focused on only that flaring heat. Here one does not need abstract theories about anger or elaborate ethical philosophy – just stick with the heat in one's stomach. The heat itself is our best opportunity to develop our practice of dharma.

Tame the anger by denying the heat its fuel and then watch it dissolve on its own, nearly as quickly as it flamed up, in the way that a fire retreats to its ashes. The key here is to be *very quick* at pouncing upon the heat – since anger itself is amazingly rapid, it is difficult to catch – and then to make sure that the heat *remains dissociated* with the situation's particulars. Denied that fuel, one's anger can be extinguished. Just stay focused on locating that heat. If one wishes, one can dance on its ashes, in celebration of the most important victory one can have – taming oneself.

One can do this each and every time, again and again. One can even strive for the Guinness World Record for quelling anger – don't let even one occasion slip by, that is all that matters. But you might object that some situations demand action and will benefit from the energy that anger can contribute to a resolution of a 'problem.' If you think this way, then go ahead and experiment *but only after you have demonstrated convincingly that you are an expert at extinguishing anger.* Defer any experimentation until after you have demonstrated to yourself an ability to locate and quell at will the heat of that anger in your stomach, there, again and again, until you become a yogi at this practice.

When you are able to do so, no more ugly lines will grow along the creases of your face, the karmic tracings of all of one's smiles and frowns. Further, you will spare your children from growing ugly faces as well. By such means humanity will definitely improve, which is our most important task.

The process described here is the result of a lifetime of impatience. But these too are mere words; and there are so many of them, and they bear no real accomplishment . Reading dharma has only a small effect since virtuous living requires more than a pleasant read. This is another one of the reasons why the texts claim that it takes three sets of countless aeons to gain enlightenment.

8
Managing Interruptions

There is one phenomenon so frequent that no day will go by without an opportunity to practice, and that is the phenomenon of being interrupted. The notion "interruption" itself implies self-importance and reflects our myopic investment in our immediate interests. It is good to be focused upon the things one does, and it is natural that when one takes on a task one becomes absorbed with it, conscientiously wanting to see it through to its completion. Interruptions delay that completion, and at times they can cascade to the point of leaving those tasks uncompleted and even forgotten, so any serious person is led to develop some vigilance regarding keeping interruptions in check.

But this can set us up *against* people and continually place us in a defensive position, from which it is difficult to develop a mind that is sympathetic toward others. University campuses are great places to observe this problem in action. For several decades my goal each workday was *not* to complete working through the pile of paperwork that had accumulated on my desk; instead, my goal was more modest: it was simply to keep the new paperwork that arrived that day from so burying the paperwork that was already there that the old paperwork became lost from sight, from where it risked also being lost from memory. If at the end of the day, I was able to depart the office after completing none of the paperwork that I intended to address in the morning – but with no new paperwork piled on top of it – I considered that day to be successful.

Hearing the knocks on one's door are among the many interruptions that anyone who works in an office faces. These interruptions can become continuous, and just as a new parent who must contend with a crying infant is often unable to think two thoughts in a row, so one is unable to compose any serious reflection in the wake of many interruptions. Yet, as in the chapter "How to Answer a Doorbell," one can *practice* while offering an open heart to whoever is knocking.. Every religious tradition I know of teaches this. But it is difficult to practice it for long, since it can leave one's other projects uncompleted. When my wife was a graduate student in geography, she once came home with the story of a professor who had returned from a year's sabbatical and to whose office she had gone to introduce herself. The professor addressed her by asking first, "So how have you come to complicate my life?" The comment devastated her, and she expressed a worry that she might be heading into a career that could render her similarly insensitive to others. I sometimes wonder how matters ended up for her regarding this; after our divorce she spent her academic career teaching at Naropa University in Boulder, Colorado, a place that I hope is more open to interruptions.

Managing interruptions well is another case of finding a middle path – one must be able to protect the integrity of the worthwhile projects in which one has invested oneself, and yet one must also *remain open* to any new persons who arrive on the scene. Since we cannot always accomplish both objectives, what can be a practice of remaining open while limiting fruitless exchanges? I have observed that as persons become older, some learn how to become more open to others, while others who age become more easily upset when the activities they are engaged in face derailment. One of the things I most admired about the Aboriginal people in Australia was how the older that their elders became, the *lighter*, *unburdened*, and more *open* they became. Nothing seemed to weigh them down. When we returned to the US after four years, we could not help noticing that as Americans age it is common for many of them to become more rigid and heavy. By comparison with Aboriginal people, older Americans seem to become not less but more easy to irritate. It seemed to me as if, quite literally, they (now I can say "we") were "up-tight," and I resolved to try to grow softer as I aged. What are the situations and life practices at work that produce such differences in the ways that people age, and what is it I must do, in the mundane ways that I live my daily life, to become more like the former? The mundane practices are the important ones.

All rational life requires commitment to the formal structures of one's thinking, and yet those formal structures can become a prison. One requires much perspective to keep from imprisoning oneself with *one's own* strategies, but since mere good intention is incapable of handling successfully the hundreds of challenges that one faces each day, one's practice has to become second nature – *habitual*, as it were. How does one accomplish this being mindful on an instinctive basis? Trying to will an instinctive response can be a contradictory practice, but this is the nature of much practice in Buddhism.

Anyone remotely acquainted with university life knows what it is like to greet a professor on the campus: fearful of interruptions, before attempting an unavoidable trip across campus most professors steel themselves by keeping their eyes continually focused on the ground in front of them, hoping that no one will notice them. Casual eye glances to and from friends reveal the mutual prayer that neither wishes to stop the other for civilities. I often skateboard around the campus, not only because it is fun but also because it provides me with a built-in excuse for getting past a colleague with nothing more time-consuming than a cheerful wave. On foot, it is customary to have one's greeting be brushed off with, "Sorry, I'm in a hurry," or "Excuse me, I'm late." I remember once, on the first day back on campus from a period of 15 months' field research in India, I ran into an old friend who, unable to successfully avoid my eye gaze, said to me, "Ken, it's good to see you!" as he vaulted past me down the walkway without looking back. I took no personal offense from the incident since he was simply enforcing a strategy to limit continuous interruptions.

At Sera Monastery, the monks are very skilled at greeting others sincerely, much more skilled than I am. For me, I'm thrilled to be able to work on my studies and translations without my door continually receiving knocks. That silence is an act of mercy, and I developed a daily routine that was quite suitable to me. I rose at 6 am with the very final bell for the monk's morning prayers and debate session, and I would grind and brew a fresh cup of local South Indian coffee, and then work for three hours on my translation. Work that requires concentration is performed especially well before one's blood is diverted to one's stomach to digest what one has eaten for breakfast, since all of one's blood can be used to oxygenate the brain. The coffee further enhances the sharpness of one's mind. It is really splendid working that way, though it has a lifespan of not much more than an hour or two. But I settled into a routine that made the most of it.

My problem with this routine was that since the Indian electric grid in rural India is shut down with the sunrise each morning at 6 am, I was forced to work directly next to the window in order to get sufficient light to shine on the pages of my Tibetan manuscript. This placed me in the field-of-view of the custodial woman of the monastery's guesthouse, who came by each morning at 6:30 am on her regular morning round of sweeping the walkways while she listened to MP-3 recordings of teachings by His Holiness the Dalai Lama. I do not mind at all the sound of the recordings, since His Holiness' voice is splendid. I've had nearly 500 hours of teachings from His Holiness myself, and it is always an inspiration to me. However, this fine woman who was undertaking her chores always wanted to engage me in some friendly Tibetan conversation. Quite wonderfully, she performed her work not simply as a job but in a dharmic way, i.e. for the sake of others. And I was one of those others who ennobled her work; so she was eager to offer me some of her kindness. The problem was that she knew I spoke Tibetan, and so she always sought some casual conversation from me, at that very early hour that I was reaching my peak mental sharpness for the entire day!

So there I was, reading an intricate Tibetan text that explains how to develop compassion (and keeping an eye on locating skillful ways to translate it into English), when instead of investing the morning's freshness and the caffeine-fired mental energy into the text, I was invited – compelled, in fact – to spend five minutes (it would be longer if I did not insist upon withdrawing) in small talk. Instead of reading about compassion I was being forced to actually practice it for five minutes! And it happened every single morning. I learned to keep the curtains drawn, but that was an undeserved insult to this kind woman and it rendered the manuscript too dim to read clearly at that early hour. Would not each opportunity to give five minutes of kindness to this cheerful fellow human have been an opportunity to practice what I was reading?

The custodian was an extraordinary person. She was strong both emotionally and physically, and she was bright. What is more, she was a determined practitioner, and in truth had made more progress than I had. In fact, we both recognized that we were up to the same business: trying to expand our capacity for practicing the dharma. And so we were compatriots in the best possible way.

The first day I arrived from abroad, the day I was installed in this uniquely solitary room as a token of the esteem that the monastery had for me, as soon as I had moved in all of my boxes and suitcases full of books, manuscripts, and dictionaries, and according to my own practice of geomancy had arranged them in the most convenient manner, the custodian knocked on my door to explain to me that the room belonged to her. She was joking, testing me perhaps, but I did not know that since her deadpan was so perfect; nevertheless, I was not at all upset. I replied that I was simply following directions and was not a decision-maker in the matter. In fact, I was so happy to be back at Sera at last that my mood was buoyant. I think my being unflappable won over her regard. Her daughter had sympathy for my confusion and explained that her mother was teasing. How cool is that: testing the foreign practitioner's dharma!

The pathetic part about this is that even someone I respect, someone who immediately is willing to become my teacher, a friend and compatriot from the very first moment – even her! – is someone with whom I do not want to have a conversation first thing in the morning. I mean to say, I am unable to display joy to greet another person *even when* joy is the response that naturally arises in my heart upon seeing her!

So then I had to face the question regarding how to strategically convert this new situation into the path. I knew that if I resolved to waste the five best minutes of each morning in unnecessary small talk, my attempt would fail and the resentment that I (and eventually she) would feel would be worse than my not making the attempt. So I settled on the following pathetic strategy: keeping the blinds half-opened (and half-closed) and being willing to engage in a short conversation every *other* day – not never, but not every day either. Not only was this less offensive, it gave me a chance to practice some mundane loving kindness one day out of two. How hard can it really be – wishing a fellow human being well at the start of a day?

9
How to Treat A Taxi Driver

On any given day, the world is filled with people who have failed to tame their minds and who find themselves engaged in contests with other similarly ignorant persons. One can laugh or one can cry, and of course we ourselves are those ignorant people. Look about any city: we ignoramuses confront each other, as if the blind were trying to guide the blind. Narrow-minded competition abounds, and unnecessary conflict is to be witnessed everywhere. When properly considered, it will break your heart.

Who will teach us how unnecessary these struggles are? Who will take responsibility for leading mundane interactions out of their narrow scope to a larger-hearted and more shared perspective? Even when we are aware of acting foolishly, we are powerless to extricate ourselves from our entanglements.

I had rented a taxi for the day in Bangalore since I had several appointments all over the city, in connection with some research I was doing with Indian colleagues. Drawing taxi drivers is a bit like drawing cards in poker, and you never know what sort of driver you will get. My driver was a very young one, who seemed diligent about his work. Though he was not born in Bangalore, he knew the city well enough, although he did not speak English and my Kannada consists of little more than "Hello, welcome," "Please come in," and "Good-bye." We were never sure of what the other was saying, and the scope for misunderstanding was adding more stress to our already difficult task of finding places that neither of us had ever visited before.

An odd phenomenon that can occur in conversations between people who do not share the same language is that when any difficulty in communication occurs, one of the parties will begin to speak more loudly, thinking that this will help to make the meaning more clear. Naturally, it encourages the other party to raise the voice as well, and before long the conversation becomes a shouting match. This is ignorance at work.

As it happened, my driver and I got lost en route to the second of my five appointments. Since I had at least planned the schedule so that I would arrive at each one a bit early, the stress of missing an important appointment had not yet arisen, so I could afford to attend to any tension I myself might be adding to our interaction. Attending to the tension one introduces is an important dharma practice.

It seemed that the driver felt that the address I had given him bore some irremediable internal contradiction, and he tried to explain to me the nature of the impossibility I had presented to him. Since his English was poor (though better than my Kannada), I was unable to grasp his point. So he spoke more loudly. After some minutes of further driving around without success, his own shouting was causing him to become increasingly upset. He pulled the car over to turn his body around and better explain to me our problem, but by then his speech had become yelling, and I felt myself close to getting sucked into his energy. Fortunately, I realized that this would contribute little to the situation, so instead of shouting back to him, I stretched both hands outward - palms facing the floor with my fingers spread apart - and said "Calm, calm. Easy going, we will find a solution," nodding softly.

The driver nodded too, lowered his voice, and we worked out a strategy for searching for our location. During the rest of the day, some six hours and four more appointments, he never raised his voice again. It was not that I was wise to respond in that way, I was just lucky.

Part of my luck was that five days previously I had an odd but relevant interaction with a customs officer at the Doha airport in Qatar. I had come off of a 15 hour flight from San Francisco, which in turn had been preceded by a flight from San Diego to San Francisco that was delayed due to mechanical difficulties, and then further delayed by fog. When I finally arrived in the Doha airport I was utterly exhausted, my bags had been lost, and I stumbled into the airport passport and security lanes to have my carry-on luggage screened. I took out my computer, put it in a bin, and placed my pack and wallet in another bin and sent it through. The officers tried to compel me to go through the metal detector portal, but since I wear a pacemaker, which I have had some problems with, my doctors have asked me not to pass through these detectors and to always request a manual search. Most airports in the Third World do not bother with manual inspections; instead, they ask for your medical card and then wave you through without examination. Doha was no different.

I explained to the officer that I had a pace-maker and showed him the pace-maker under my shirt. He yelled out, "Card! Card! You have card?!" I nodded, "Yes." "Well, show card!" I explained, "My card is with my wallet that is in the machine." He acted as if he didn't hear me, probably because he didn't comprehend my English, since he said again angrily, "I said show card!" I yelled back in return, "Yes! Yes! My card is in the machine!"

He stood up and scolded me, "Why you yell?! Why you yell?! Don't yell. Show card now!" It seems he didn't understand my words and was upset that I had raised my voice, which I had indeed done, in just the way my taxi driver would do later. I pointed to the machine and said, "My card is there!"

Finally he seemed to understand, but he gave priority to his explaining to me that it was unnecessary to yell. He wanted some recognition of his authority, or at least his humanity. I spoke softly, "I'm sorry. My card is there, in my wallet," pointing again. He went over to the machine, handed me my wallet, and I took out my medical card and showed it to him. He said, "Good, O.K. But stop yelling."

The customs officer was right. Though he had been a contributor, what was I to gain by entering a yelling contest with an officer of a foreign country? It was sheer stupidity, but traveling is difficult work, and I was unable to catch any sleep on the planes. As I passed by him, I thanked him for his "good lesson" and admitted, "I shouldn't yell." This made him extremely happy, and he suddenly became eager to help guide me to the correct next step. Now new-found friends, I told him that I had a son who works in Doha and who speaks Arabic, and this made him even happier. I am sure he is not the only customs officer who has tried to educate loud, often proud, Americans. It must be a difficult job, but someone has to do it. I passed through without any body examination.

With this lesson fresh in my mind, I was better able to catch myself just about to engage in a contest with my Bangalore taxi driver. We really do have a responsibility to *initiate* some kindness. Someone has to start the process. And it works best when one can be kind without any sense of moral superiority. Even when one is able to freeze one's egotistic competitiveness mid-conversation, one can then develop some pride regarding the ability to do so, and thus the egotism manages to survive in tact enough to hinder the interaction. That is how subtle egotism can be.

Egotism can become more subtle still, such as mine now: I do not have pride regarding my ability to calm overly exercised conversations for the good reason that my ability to do this is nill; instead, my pride now lies in my confessing how pathetic I am. Our egotism is harder to shake than our shadow. When I confess how pathetic I am to my students, they usually think I am merely being polite; only the students who know me well know that the truth of the matter is that I really don't know much about how to calm a tense interaction.

So long as there is ego at work, one will find it difficult to teach anything. Since the ignorant people who keep contesting each other are usually jealous about guarding their egos, even when one tries to calm a situation without egoism, others may read egotism into it. Yes, counseling calmness can be another way to show off or to retain control of an interaction. Even when there is no ego at work, the other person's jealousy may be projected into the situation and produce an identical result, rendering all remedies ineffective and progress impossible. We are every bit this pathetic, since jealousy motivates the preponderance of human interactions. As Langri Senge has told us in his "Thought Transformation in Eight Stanzas,"

> When others, out of jealousy,
> treat me badly with abuse, insults and the like,
> I shall accept their hard words
> and ... view them as my spiritual friend.

Similarly, Shantideva has advised us about difficult people, "Hold this dear one who is so difficult to find as though one has discovered a precious treasure." A taxi driver who abuses us, for whatever reason, is our teacher because he tests our progress in taming our minds. A taxi driver who is reasonable offers us no training in dharma. My taxi driver was just right – he was not so unreasonable that I became self-righteously indignant, but his lack of wisdom was enough to test my own wisdom, and by meeting this test I could cultivate my wisdom further. Anyone who causes us to cultivate wisdom this way is our teacher.

A few days later in Mysore I was less successful with a rickshaw driver. I had arrived by a train that had been delayed for two hours. It was an especially crowded train station in Bangalore since it was a holiday period, and the railway cars were unbelievably stuffed with people whose patience had been exhausted (even for Indians who have more patience than most people do). I rode to my friend's home, where we chatted for a couple of hours. Then we went to his parents' home for dinner. Since I had a large suitcase, my friend arranged a second rickshaw for me, told the driver where to take me, and said he would meet us at the home. His instructions were in Kannada, so I was unable to follow them. It seems it was on Ramanujan Road, but the numbered cross street was lost to me, since I don't know my Kannada numbers beyond three.

The rickshaw driver stopped at 9th Cross, and said that this was where he was told to take me; however, my friend was not there. It was dark and getting late, and I had nowhere else to go. I told the driver I did not know where to go. But I was calm. I thought to myself, "Well, for sure I will survive this even if it has to be in a hotel. So why get upset?" Pretty good, thus far.

The driver asked if I had my friend's telephone number. I did, and I gave it to the driver, who had his own cell phone (I do not own one). I showed him the numbers as I read them aloud. He dialed, but there was no connection. We tried it again, but still there was no response, and my driver informed me that my number was "no good." Since I knew it was the correct number, I asked to see his cell phone. Even though I do not know the first thing about cell phones, I could see the number that had just been dialed, and the driver had transposed two separate pairs of numbers. I had drawn a driver who had dyslexia! Not only had he taken me to the wrong cross (9th Cross instead of 14th Cross, as it turned out), he was unable to dial a number without mixing up the digits. Exhausted past my resolve to be a bodhisattva, I scolded him.

He dialed the correct number, received the instructions a second time, and at last I arrived at the destination. As we rode, I asked myself why I scolded him. How would that energy make any contribution to his dyslexia? For 16 years I had a wife with a mild form of dyslexia, and my castigations only contributed to our divorce, so I should have learned. Surely I am one of the ignoramuses of which I speak. But on those occasions when we don't get it right, we can still engage in a constructive practice: we can reflect upon our mistaken ways. So as we rode in the night air through the dark Mysore streets, I considered how I still have much work before I know how to treat a taxi driver properly.

The key point here is that we are responsible for the emotions of the people we meet.

When faced with undeserved conflict, instead of becoming angry it is best to celebrate the opportunity to practice. If we cope with it without egotism, there are occasions when we can accomplish a bit of good, for others and for ourselves. If it should happen that one is successful in taming a hostile situation, one should accept no credit for oneself since that will only resurrect the egotism at another level.

For sure, let us also dedicate the merit of any lucky victory to the welfare of those innocent souls who continue to contest each other each day, without offering each other any relief.

II

Methods for the Mundane

10
Writing Student Recommendations

Being a university professor requires that one be skilled in many disparate tasks. It is like being a circus master, but instead of three rings, there are a baker's dozen: scholar, psychological counselor, lecturer/performer, grade negotiator, committee member, fund-raiser, writer, research coordinator, community consultant, journal editor, multimedia software designer, library advocate, etc. The reason that professors tend towards absent-mindedness is that they are required to keep current many varieties of tasks that share little in common with each other. One has to recall the quiz that must be duplicated, the committee report that must be signed by the department head, the article whose revision had to be completed by a month previous, a book that still needs reading (preferably before one writes the lecture) – and so on. It is difficult to keep these many different agendas in play without missing one or two beats.

Amidst this plethora of job tasks are the recommendations that one composes on behalf of students. These are recommendations for undergraduates looking for scholarships for summer abroad programs, recent graduates looking for employment, colleagues applying for fellowships, and postdoctoral students who are addicted to surfing the internet for grants they have not yet applied for. Although they seem to come bunched a few times each year (especially November to January), they can arrive at any time, most usually just a few days before the deadline for sending them. And many of them require a good deal of thought, for it is my experience that any letter less than two pages will not taken be seriously by a funding agency; and to be believed one has to find that right balance between praise and criticism. The hackneyed paragraphs common in recommendations are obvious to anyone who has to read through stacks of them, and so writing a good recommendation that will capture the reviewer's attention requires serious work.

One interesting aspect to writing recommendations is that it is not normally something that provides any benefits for oneself. One does not receives credit for them when one's job performance is being evaluated; in fact, on most occasions one never hears again from the student concerned, whether or not the recommendation was successful. This makes them a perfect item for dharma practice: one is ensured of not benefiting by one's kindness!

For my first decade as a professor, I would silently roll my eyes upward when the most recent batch of requests for recommendations arrived: "Another holiday weekend lost!" would be my immediate thought. One year I had gone on unpaid leave the entire ten-week winter term of my university employment in order to spend time writing a book. The price I paid to get the time to write my book was one-third of my annual salary. Despite this fact, I spent the entire month of January absorbed in writing student recommendations. The students did not get the memo that I was on leave.

As I grew older I came to appreciate that many of the people concerned were students that I cared for; otherwise, they probably would not have asked me for the recommendation. I realized that if I transformed my attitude, I could wallow in a bit of loving kindness and write some very effective letters for people that I cared about. In this way I managed to turn a chore into a celebration of sorts. I will not claim that I now look forward to writing recommendations, but I can say that on occasion I have been able to turn the activity into a wholesome experience that is capable of improving my character.

It took a while for me to be successful at this. Sometimes the requests for recommendations arrive at the least convenient times. I have received the requests at 12,000 feet in the Himalayas, while tramping through a Central American jungle (and serendipitously stumbling into an internet connection), in Patagonia, and in remote deserts of Mexico. Nevertheless, I do my best to view them as opportunities for cultivating the precious *bodhicitta* attitude – because that way I am the chief beneficiary. Some days I become absorbed into pouring out my kindness on behalf of my students, and what greater reason for joy can there be for a person who claims to be a professor? But on other days I do fail miserably.

Oddly as it seems, the best part of this change of policy is that I am less burdened by the unpleasant aspects of the chore, and its heaviness has mostly evaporated. In its place I experience feelings that are lighter to bear. Success in life may consist of transforming each of our chores in a similar way. Living lightly is better than living with heaviness.

11
Generosity

Many basic Mahayana texts suggest that of all the ethical practices of a bodhisattva, generosity is the easiest one to practice. That is why it is the first among the six perfections. It is also a practice that is recommended by many texts about mind-transformation, along with the additional advice that those who are unfamiliar with generosity but are desirous of increasing their compassion should practice first by showing kindness to the people with whom they are the closest. Perhaps even more than to a spouse, one feels warmly toward one's children; accordingly, one can most easily commence a practice of generosity with them. Here is how I learned to practice this way.

We live in an age where some parents order their children out of the house at maturity, or charge them rent, or are stingy about their contributions to their offspring's college education. It may be tough love, or it may be selfishness, and on occasion the two motives may coincide. But since the love that a parent can have for a child is very great, it is still the easiest way to begin a successful practice of generosity. Of course, wanton generosity can spoil a child, and harm can be done by setting up an environment in which a child feels entitled to everything received from the hands of the parents' generosity. Above all, Buddhist practice requires skill-in-means. Frequently, what heals can act as poison, so one must give wisely. As always, motivation is important in these matters.

I have been blessed with a grateful, considerate son, who has never taken my generosity for granted; moreover, he is modest in his pursuit of his pleasures. Upon his graduation with honors, he was truly tired of the stress to perform to the highest expectations, a burden under which he labored since commencing high school. He was resolved about not attending graduate school; instead, he hoped to go into the foreign service. He had come close to being hired right out of college by several US governmental agencies, but it was to be a number of years before he finally ended up working at the State Department. After an internship at the Brookings Institution, he found employment in the private sector as an investigator of the viability of markets for new products and services. He worked in both English and Spanish, and it was an experience from which he learned a great deal. It paid well, and during the first year, he managed to save more than $12,000.

A son like that makes it easy to be confident that generous assistance will be marshaled well. When he was still in middle school, I made a promise to him that no matter what it took to pay for his undergraduate studies, I would see to it that he would graduate without owing a dime to anyone. This was partly my response to my own father, who steadfastly refused to contribute anything to my college education, despite owning a handsome home in Beverly Hills. In raising my son, much of the time I relied upon a strategy of doing just the opposite of what my own father would have done (some of our childhood wounds can be healed by our own practices of parenting). In my promise, I added a provision that it would be my expectation that graduate studies or any professional studies would be undertaken on his own resources. I kept my promise, which required my spending a healthy portion of the profit from the sale of my Oregon house in paying off his assembled college loans. After it was done, I had only modest resources, but I felt free, and during the two years following his graduation, my son did not ask me for financial assistance.

After eighteen months in the private sector, my son began to think that graduate studies were not so bad after all. He wisely concluded that he needed further training in international economics, and in Arabic. So he applied to four first-rate graduate schools, two of them in the Washington, D.C. area (Georgetown and Johns Hopkins), and I helped him with his applications. He informed me that he would be using his substantial savings for tuition, but that they would not quite cover one-half of his expenses for the first year of study, so he asked me to help out. I replied that it would be impossible for me to refuse, though my resources were small. I recognized that this was another opportunity for me to cultivate a bit of honest generosity, for if I was unable to be generous with my son, what hope would there be for me to be generous with others?

What is honest generosity? It is generosity that (1) really costs something, and (2) is performed without any thought of getting something in return. During the months when I was not teaching (for five years I had a semi-retirement contract under which I taught for only three months a year), I was living on a pension of $1760 a month, from which an expensive health insurance policy had to be paid. With these limited resources and his real needs, what was the solution?

I resolved to help in the following way. I taught a class during the summer term, for which my profit, after taxes and living expenses in Eugene, was $3,000. I sent him the three thousand as a gift. Five weeks of sweat and blood of a father for his son is nothing more than the way of the world. And such labor can be performed with an eye toward the virtue that one always accrues by dedicating the fruits of one's labors to another person. That in this case the other person is one's only son makes it a meek act of generosity. But performed in the right way, i.e. with total dedication and a motive for holding on to nothing, it can build some character just the same. And that should be job-one: locating more opportunities for building the bodhisattva character. It will turn the activity into a project that fosters joy.

At the same time, I decided to set aside an additional $3,000 during the subsequent three month-long spring term when I would be working as a university professor at full salary (then $5,000 per month, after taxes), but that would not be gifted. It would be an explicit loan, so that some sense of the real limitation of resources and a reciprocity of obligation is also taught. My $6,000 all together was no more than 20% of my son's expenses, so it was too modest a figure to be made into a boast. He had already have saved close to 50%, and received some small assistance from his mother and maternal grandfather, making the amount left for undertaking the obligation of a formal loan not overwhelmingly burdensome.

The good sense that motivates these acts is considerably less than the wisdom of Solomon; nevertheless, it was a virtuous practice to undertake. The heart of the practice was working each day with the awareness that no personal financial benefit will be reaped. This turned those weeks of labor into a practice of renunciation, which is the first of the three principal aspects of the path.

12
"Prego!" and Other Common Courtesies

There is nothing more vital for living the good life than sharing common sentiments with our fellow beings. It is obvious that a newborn receives as much nurture from being loved as it does from food, and it is amazing how all animals arrive already prepared to love. There is nothing that makes us more human than our capacity to share sentiments, to absorb the gentle warmth and fond acceptance that others offer us. Although the society of late consumer capitalism has become a me-first, myopic project, we find real happiness only when we relinquish that individualism and receive sustenance from participation in the collective sentiments of our social group.

Accomplishing this requires that we cultivate some capacity to tune in to other peoples' ways of being. If we exclusively use other people as tools for assisting our own purposes, we may satisfy those objectives but we will never come to know the high peace that inhabits the hearts of those who stop and tune in to the sentiments of others. In fact, the difference between a *bodhisattva* and an ordinary person (nicknamed "mere child" in the Tibetan language) is that ordinary persons pursue only their own interests (*rang don*), whereas *bodhisattva*-s spend all of their time tuning in to the being and sentiments of others (*gshan don*). That is, a *bodhisattva* cherishes other people while ordinary persons cherish mostly themselves. Happily, each of the world's cultures has developed an arsenal of social habits that foster genuine relations with others. These go by the name of civilities, and while in our time they are considered to be of minor consequence, they offer guidance for those who would like to more regularly tap into the peace that comes from social solidarity.

It may not be necessary to do all of the talking in order to tap into that peace. It may even be the case that listening can be more effective. At least that was always the advice of my wife and son. The irony is that people who talk a great deal may *never* discover the fact that greater happiness can come from being quiet in a group of people, receiving collective sentiments without having to dominate them. Only a shallow pleasure comes from controlling others. I know this so well because I am one of those who fail to offer much space to others.

There is a common practice among Italians that is used by them to surrender some social space to a fellow fraternizer. From time to time it happens that someone with whom one is sitting has a need for something – the person may want to pour another cup of coffee for herself, grab an apple, pass by to a seat closer to the fire, etc. When such a need arises, the person may request permission, as in "May I move closer to the fire?" When such a request for broadening the personal space over which a person has authority has been made, an Italian will answer, "*Prego!*" which means "Please!" or "Kindly extend the sphere of your personal discretion until you are satisfied." This "*Prego!*" is always uttered with an exclamation point and some agreeable eye-to-eye contact. Occasionally, it is accompanied by a slight gesture of one hand (palm upward) that implies generosity. Tibetans have a similar gesture, but they do it with both hands without uttering any words; they use the same gesture when they make offerings to a buddha. What distinguishes both of these is the intimation that the generosity has no limitations. Moreover, the tone of the Italian, "*Prego!*" carries the sweetest communing with another, and it is used as an opportunity for cementing the social bond. More than politeness, it is an admission that one's own well being is always dependent upon the well being of one's associate.

The American novelist Cormac McCarthy has described this situation with accuracy, and speaking of Mexicans McCarthy writes, "And after and for a long time to come he'd have reason to evoke the recollection of those smiles and to reflect upon the good will which provoked them for it had power to protect and to confer honor and to strengthen resolve and it has power to heal men and to bring them to safety long after all other resources were exhausted."[1] "Honor" is the correct word here because these social sentiments are embodied in ancient social routines that have evolved under the labels honor, civility, and courtesy. They acknowledge the interdependence of humans, an interdependence that indeed "has power to heal." Perhaps it is the only thing that has the power to heal.

The Kannadigas of the south central Indian state of Karnataka, fifty million of them, have developed their own gesture of camaraderie. When they wish to reference a developing social bond, they will place their right hand over their heart as they speak, as if to gift one's heart to one's companion. It is the sweetest of gestures, one that announces an absence of malice and a readiness to tune in to the other. Each of us has a power to create others as a reflection of our own energy, and we need to accept this responsibility seriously: whatever social actions may result, it is for sure that the attitude that we ourselves have brought to the interaction has been responsible for it. When we give hostility, we receive hostility; when we bequeath the space to be, we receive more space in return. There will always be enough oxygen for everyone to breathe, so there is no need to constantly try to consume all the air in a room, suffocating everyone. Being with another does not always require talking constantly.

---

[2] Cormac McCarthy, *All the Pretty Horses*, p. 219.

The Aboriginal people of Australia, with whom I lived for two years, were the people most skilled at being with each other that I have ever known. Their natural pastime is to consider, each and every moment, how other people are really feeling. The reasons they may have developed such expertise are many – they live together in small groups of people, without houses, with whom they will interact throughout their lives (so they cannot treat people lightly since they are stuck with each other until they die); they have an oral culture and so social intercourse is less mediated by abstractions; they are not invested in their personal identities, but derive their identities from their social solidarity (it was Durkheim's study of Australian Aborigines that led him to conceive of the term "social solidarity"); etc. I have never been with people who are more tuned-in to the intimate feelings of whichever person they are with. It is a joy just to share their consociality, and it is not necessary to utter a single word.

When my friends and colleagues hear me speak this way, they conclude that I am a hopeless romantic, and that what I am describing is a projection of my sentimentalism. It is not! There really exist *genuine differences* in the form of the consociality of the peoples around the world, and not all people are the same. It is simply a fact that Americans are more self-absorbed and self-centered than are some other people in the world. There are even some good things that accompany the American vice, since independence, individualism, civil rights and liberties, are all products that accompany the sovereign individualism of modern American life.

During the years I lived among Tibetans, I occasionally heard an odd neologism that translates as "the me-first people" (*nga dang po gi mi*). I did not understand what it was supposed to mean until one day I asked a friend about it who laughed, and he embarrassedly explained to me that it was a term that some Tibetans use to refer to Americans. In Buddhism there are "the three precious jewels" (the Buddha, the doctrines of compassion and emptiness (also known as *dharma*), and the community of diligent aspirants); but there also exist the three non-precious jewels, which are said to be "me, myself, and I." That Tibetans sometimes refer to Americans as the me-first people implies that the level of self-assertiveness that is second nature in contemporary American cities is an identifying cultural feature, and so real differences in cherishing self and cherishing others do exist across societies.

In Mexico, there are people who are Hispanic in race and heritage and people who are indigenous, and there is every combination of the two. In the district of northern Mexico where I live, the persons born and raised there have a background that stems from the Spanish, English, Italian, and even Swedish settlers that landed in Baja California more than a century ago (the original inhabitants died of diseases during the first decades of Spanish colonization). Socialized in the Spanish way, they have a highly formalized language of courtesy, during which they always inquire about the welfare of each person they meet, even strangers. They will commence even a casual interaction with "*Como esta?*" ("How are you doing?") and to this, their associate is required to reply and inquire in turn: "*Bien, gracias. Como esta usted?*" This is a standard device of social interaction that Mexicans regularly use to cultivate a fellow feeling with another.

Some Americans who visit here find this delay in proceedings to be an unnecessary inconvenience, and they may attempt to skip past it. I have heard them interrupt the civilities with "Yah, yah, what I need is ..." One winter my tank had run out of propane gas and with strong rains being forecast I was worried that the heavy gas trucks would soon be unable to navigate the muddy road to my house; therefore, I kept a close eye out for any truck making deliveries of gas. One day I waited all morning without one coming, but in the afternoon I heard the truck, and I ran out to catch it before it had gone by. Gesticulating wildly, I caught the attention of the driver and directed him to where the tank was standing on my property. Once he had arrived and stepped out of the truck, instead of looking into his eyes, offering the customary greeting, and establishing some fellow feeling, I attempted to lead him to the valve of the tank. He stood where he was and said to me, "No." I turned back, and asked "*Que dice?*" ("What are you saying?"). He replied that the proper way to interact was for me to ask him how he was feeling ("*Como esta?*") and to exchange sufficient pleasantries to indicate that I recognized his humanity. He said that that was more important than the business transaction. What a fabulous teaching! In short, I was being a brute, and was being called out for it by the Mexican who was sticking up for the civility of his culture.

The indigenous people of Mexico are in even less of a hurry, a trait that has made it vulnerable for the racist humor of American comedy. In this part of northern Mexico a majority of the people were born in southern Mexico. On our rancho there is an extended family of people from Oaxaca, whose first language is not Spanish. They are a reliable group of folks who do much of the necessary labor required by the gringos who reside on the ranch. They are honest and adept at solving problems, but they work more slowly than do those Mexicans who are more acculturated to European and American ways. They are almost *never* in a hurry, whereas most Americans seem to be in a hurry. The Americans and even the more Hispanic Mexicans are often critical of the pace at which Oaxacans work. They never deny that they work diligently, but it seems that the Oaxacans are reluctant to allow their work tasks to harass them to the point of becoming stressed. As the saying goes, "Only mad dogs and Englishmen work in the noonday sun."

I am reminded of a time in the US wheh I was in a hurry to grab a cup of gourmet coffee from an espresso café. I went up to the counter and found a barista who was engaged in an extended conversation with a customer that he had already served. He saw me waiting for the several minutes while he completed his discussion; after some minutes, he unapologetically walked over with a slow but deliberate pace, in order to ask me for my order. Although my impatience must have been obvious to him, he retained total calm and did not hurry; he did not allow my "rush" energy to have the slightest influence upon his temporality or demeanor. It was his own dharma practice. I told him that he was not my barista; rather, he was my teacher. What a fabulous sense of calm self-control he demonstrated.

The other day I was talking with my neighbor about some work he had been doing on a new garage. He was using one of the younger Oaxacans to help him with his project. I knew myself that this young man was inexpensive to hire but slow in his labor. I had once observed him paint the flashing of another structure, a task that I could have completed in a few hours, and it took him two days, despite the fact that he was being paid for the job and not by the hour. At the time I had joked that he does not like to apply more paint to an adjacent area until all of the paint that was just applied to the previous section had dried. Regarding this laborer, I asked my neighbor, "So how is Alfonso working out?" My neighbor replied, "Wonderful. I've learned more from him about how to work without being stressed than from anyone I have ever worked with. He allows nothing to disrupt his serenity."

These energies that accompany the most mundane occasions are vitally important for the quality of our lives. When one takes some time, it is more likely that one will be able to contribute to the fellow feeling that we can share with others. Where does this much time exist?

Another neighbor of mine knows impatience exclusively; moreover, he moves quickly to dominate every interaction that he has with another person. When he drives, he insists upon being the commander of the highway, and any driver who interferes with him receives his scorn. What is worse, he usually justifies his priority with principles: the other driver is not only in his way, he is employing driving practices that are morally flawed! The result is that this neighbor knows little peace, and he rarely becomes familiar with the joy of letting others be – in their own way – nor does he have very much familiarity the fellow feeling that such letting-be can breed. He may consider himself a "winner," but he is so lost in his praxis of continuous self-assertion that he is unable to recognize that he is losing out. What is worse, he leaves disharmony in his wake, as if a tornado has just passed through the neighborhood. Instead of this, our goal should be to contribute harmony. How do we learn to do that?

How do we learn to slow down enough to tune in to our friends? How do we retain the calm and maximize the charity, while minimizing the "rush"? There exist at our disposal a number of congenial social conventions that can assist us, conventions like "*Prego!*" or "*Como esta!*" It is possible that Brazilians even exceed Mexicans when it comes to offering heart-felt greetings. Instead of asking how one is in a friendly but emotionally neutral way, the Brazilians wax enthusiastic when they greet their fellows with their "*Tudo bem?!!!*" When I asked my Brazilian friend to write down the spelling of it, he added the three exclamation marks; and then, without my asking he wrote the English translation underneath, "Is it all O.K.!" using only one exclamation mark. I told him, "Yes, you have it right - the "*Tudo bem*" exceeds the 'O.K.' in its gusto by about a 3:1 ratio, and that captures nearly perfectly the difference between the two cultures." He laughed and nodded. It is like the difference between shaking hands with one hand or with both hands – in the latter case the engagement of the heart is more sustained. Where Mexicans insist on eye contact, Brazilians insist on both eye contact and some genuine enthusiasm. This is the real work of living, and is a practice compatible with Buddhist dharma.

The practice of placing one's palm over one's heart as is done in Karnataka, India, or extending both hands as the Tibetans do, palms facing upwards with a slight movement toward the other as if to gift others space for their own being, are also Buddhist practices. These are very old traditions that were developed by humans in times that were much slower than our own. Instead of treating these practices as inefficient, backward and dispensable, we can learn to employ them in ways that enhance our capacity for feeling kindly toward others, and for demonstrating that feeling so that it can be recognizable by others. Or we can develop our own traditions of hospitality and solicitous concern. In all cases, it is the motivation that one directs toward the other person that counts most. And it is simple to do: the secret is to care. In most places in the world that I've visited, this *is* what is meant by spiritual.

13

Offering the Victory to Others

Many years ago, when I was a junior professor, I gave my students in Tibetan Buddhism a class assignment that required that they observe the most mundane events of their day and locate a situation where they found themselves embroiled in some competition with other persons for space, service, or a turn of some kind. The assignment required them to apply the advice of Geshe Chekawa, who suggested, "Offer the victory to the other."

This assignment required that for one moment they suspend their competitive drive to obtain some sought-for prize (a parking place, a turn at the photocopying machine, service in a café, etc.). Their task was to consider the difference that surrendering the opportunity might have made, and they had to summarize the events and their feelings in a three-page paper.

It was my intention that my students gain some practical experience with this sage advice from the Kadampa tradition – to give the victory to the other – and thereby learn that happiness does not lie in obtaining or not obtaining mundane objectives. The result was quite the opposite. Most of the students' papers expressed strong resentment at having to surrender an opportunity to another person. More than a few were unable to release their fixation upon their desired aim, and they expressed they were even more displeased that such an undeserving person should be made the beneficiary of their sacrifice. It seemed that in my class generosity of spirit was in short supply.

Somehow, word of this assignment made its way to the Dean's office, and during our next meeting he suggested that the assignment approached closely the practice of religion, something that must be avoided in the university. He said to me, "This assignment seems innocuous, but you need to be careful. Our task here is to study religion, not to practice it." I replied to my Dean, "Oh, don't worry. I would never do anything that could possibly improve the character of our students." Indeed, the results of my experiment with the advice of Geshe Chekawa proved that it was not at all easy to improve people's character. It may that Americans are so steeped in their self-absorbed individualism that more than a course on Tibetan Buddhism is required.

What more is the serious question.

At the most basic level of ordinary daily Buddhist practice is a prayer that has as its climax the offering of a visualized mandala. One interlaces the fingers of one's hand in a unique fashion that represents Mt. Meru and the four worlds that represents the material universe, and one lifts one's hands formed in this mandala up in front of one's heart and offers it – and all of one's possessions, desires, and abilities, which is what the mandala is meant to represent – to others. The mandala offering accompanies most elementary prayers, and it is said that what is important is to keep working at the quality of one's mandala offering. That quality needs to be polished like silverware.

Of course in any religion most rituals are largely done by rote, with the externals performed with perfect obsequiousness without causing much internal transformation. But if one really lets go of one's possessions, desires, etc. and thinks of others benefitting from them, recollecting that one should enhance the experience of others, then despite its remoteness from reality it is an effective practice. It all comes down to the sincerity of the generosity that one tenders. Working on a genuine mandala offering is not an easy obligation to fulfill, but when one is able to cultivate the right motivation, it does make one's heart lighter.

Being a poor practitioner, I can sometimes offer one mandala in the proper way each day, which is a practice I cherish, but some of the longer tantric practices require meditative recitations that require a dozen mandala offerings, sometimes one to each deity that sits at each chakra (the heart, the throat, the head, the solar plexus, the genitalia, etc.), and after the third or forth mandala offering, it is nearly impossible for me to sustain genuine motivation. Western students of Buddhism usually want the highest level of tantric initiation, but they are not so well prepared for the multiplication of mandala offerings that are entailed. I once asked my teacher, the Sera Je Abbot Lobsang Tsering, why they have us do so many mandala offerings, one after the other, and why one or two each day would not be sufficient. He laughed heartily, and he considered my question to be so absurd that he retold a story about it to many of his students, as an illustration of how difficult it is for Westerners to understand tantric practice. A younger student of the Abbot that I met for the first time years later told me, "Oh, you're the one that the story was about!"

Mandala offerings are a terrific practice, but one has to work on the quality of one's heart while making the offering, and continuing to visualize offerings once that quality has deteriorated can become counter-productive. Such a practice should serve to recondition oneself so that one will be able to reach the point where one can "Offer the victory to the other" without the taste of regret. Transforming one's character is serious work. The pivotal aspect involves surrendering one's agenda and *making room* for the agendas of others. Some people can do this effortlessly, and others are so incapable of doing so that they fail to recognize that it is even a possibility.

The German philosopher Günter Figal, who holds the same academic chair at the University of Freiburg that was held by Edmund Husserl and Martin Heidegger, has observed that some people are naturally more aim-oriented than others, and says that gaining real insight into one's experience requires "breaking" one's aim-oriented thinking in order to give others room. Other people, he said, "have an upbringing that allows them to hold back before others' freedom and to help others be freed"; that is, being able to give the victory to others requires becoming habituated to it. With much repetition and long practice, it can become part of one's nature, but it is difficult to simply will it by one's mind, as the assignment with my students demonstrated.

Figal writes, "Heidegger describes this failure as 'insistence,' in which the human being insists 'on the protection of himself through what is accessible to him.'"[2] The result is that "instead of taking the open [i.e. what can be witnessed beyond one's concepts] as a measure, the human being now takes his measure from his own intentions and planning. In doing so, he misses himself all the more fundamentally." It is not that one is ignorant in *any* which way: one is ignorant specifically by being obsessed with the particular aims and notions that one has conceived and upon which one has fixated. Opening up here requires surrendering one's fixations. That is because one's mind has become so filled up with one's aims and projects that there is no longer any space left to see clearly, and certainly insufficient space to offer affordances for other people's freedom. This is true even when our aims and projects are worthy.

---

2 Günter Figal, *Objectivity*, New York: SUNY Press, 2010, pp. 178-79.

14
My Dune Speaks Back

During my 60s, I have been keeping two residences. One is six acres in a thickly forested wilderness (a spotted owl preserve) off the electrical grid in northern California; it has a river with cascades that rage through it, and also deep swimmable/drinkable forest-green pools. The other home is on a remote beachfront sand dune in northern Baja California, at the furthest southerly extension of the coastal chaparral plant zone. In both cases, I have been reluctant to transform the landscape or to build aggressively, believing that I first needed to learn from the land rather than try to coerce it to my vision. As the Thai Buddhist teacher Achaan Buddhadhasa said, "The forest is the teacher here." What does he mean?

I once had a newly arrived neighbor where I spent 12 years on the coast in central Oregon. He was from Pismo Beach, California, and he had just moved with his wife into the trailer home that was already sitting on the site. When his chainsaw awoke me on the very first morning after his arrival, I put on my clothes and went to investigate the noise and found this industrious Californian old-timer "clearing" a space for his house-to-be. He was sawing down the ancient trees that the local birdlife used as sentinel posts. I suggested to him that it would be nice if he could leave a few of the tall Sitka spruce standing and restrict his cutting to the shorter shorepines. He replied with firm authority, "No, they all have to go."

I suggested that he could first spend a week living there to learn what the vegetation does on its own before he starts to redesign it, an idea he accepted as ludicrous.

Finally, I suggested that he leave the largest spruce as a seed tree, and I offered him the suggestion that keeping it would help him to retain the monetary value of the land. The next day I noticed that he had taken my advice and spared the tree, but the rest of his forest looked like it had been napalmed. Six months later his wife and he divorced, and a year later he sold the property with the trailer home that had preceded him left as the only residence. Now decades have gone by, and I still sometimes pass that tree, and each time I feel some pride in having saved it from mindless destruction. Saving one grandfather Sitka spruce can be placed on the list of my life's accomplishments. I'll grant that it's not exactly Johnny Appleseed, but as a contribution it is beyond censure.

Land is not inert, and there is a kind of reflexivity to interacting with an area of wild land, and whatever one does to it usually prompts it to make some reply. That reply may be desirable or undesirable, and most of the time it is unexpected. If one cuts some Douglas fir, then oaks and alder will grow— good if you want to eat acorns, bad if you want lumber. If one plants a garden, bugs will proliferate. Let a forest grow thick, and the cool wind that has been suppressing mosquitoes will disappear. One's poor ability to anticipate what the land will do is what keeps it interesting, and educational. Turn the river into a cold storage refrigerator, and animals large and small will begin to count on your supplies. Build a room on the roof, and the downstairs will become colder during winter days. One should not dream that one's plans, *especially* those with perfectly rational designs, will not speak back in wondrous ways. The real work is in opening oneself up to a dialogue with what is wild.

This last winter I decided to build myself a little mini-beach on my property in Baja, since the daily northwest winds render the actual beach itself too cool for sun-bathing much of the year. This requires some explanation: the interior of northern Baja heats up considerably more than does the interior of coastal Alta California (the original name for what became the US State of California); however, the ocean currents between Punta Banda (just south of Ensenada) and Punta Canoas (just north of Guerrero Negro) run five to ten degrees colder than does the ocean off of the Southern California Bight (Los Angeles), which has a relatively shallow continental shelf. There is a greater temperature differential between the land and the sea in Baja California Norte than exists in Alta California. Since it is this temperature difference between a cold ocean and a hot inland that produces most of the winds, the winds are stronger where I live here in Baja than they are further north. Punta San Carlos, about a two hour's drive south of me and visible on a clear day from the top of my sand dune, is an international mecca for windsurfing.

In order to build my artificial beach, I required a small room for the exercise equipment, and I also wanted a large wall that would block the steady wind that is an uninterrupted six-month northerly blow along the lee side of my dune. I included a small window in the room that could be opened to provide some natural air conditioning on the hottest days, but it mostly remains closed. Also, I brought down many wheelbarrows of sand from higher up the dune to serve as the beach. The result was pretty; only after a decade of observing the place prior to this addition, did I invent a desirable new micro-habitat.

I went up to the States for a month to give some lectures and to visit my doctors, and when I returned I found a plume of pure clean sand running into the top corner of my artificially made beach. The wind had blown continually during the time I was gone, and the sand that was lifted into the air from the dunes by the steady northwest winds drifted out a hundred yards to my new 6'x12' room and 18' wall, and dropped its load of grains on the lee side of the wall I had built. I had placed a foot-high, flat boulder in one corner of the area to serve as a table, and the new clean plume of white sand had breached the top of that boulder. It bore the same clean wildness that the sands in a dry river bed have after the runoff of a heavy rain. It revealed the sheer nature of land everywhere, wherever gravity has its way, from the Rockies to the Himalayas, from the earth to Mars, as well as to whatever orbiting bodies of matter lie further beyond. I was grateful for the serendipitous contribution from the wildness of the sand dune to my new beach. It kept me in touch with what is universal.

I learned that there was no longer any need for me to transport sand. All I needed to do was to drag out a 2"x4" beam of wood and scrape the sand from the plume at the periphery of the "beach" into the rest if the area. So it will be a beach that will continually refresh itself, by itself, as part of the course of natural events. New tongues of wild sand show up every few weeks, which keeps placing me into a dialogue with what has remained wild. Sometimes things work out.

15
A Daily Aspiration

It is has long been my wish to overcome what the Tibetans call "the emotional afflictions" that influence my behavior, but by the time I reached the age of 60 I more or less concluded that I was not going to be able to overcome them in any comprehensive way. Nevertheless, it is part of the wisdom of old age to accept oneself even when others may not; otherwise, no peace will ever reward one's life, and progress can take place only when there is some peace stabilized in one's heart. In recent years I have set my sights lower, and now my principal daily aspiration is to prevent myself from inflicting any of my neuroses upon others.

This is an effective practice of dharma that conjoins both method and wisdom in one path. Resolving not to let the slightest dust particle from one's neuroses fall upon the mental continuity of another person is a fine gift to offer to the world. We have emotional afflictions, including neurotic obsessions, and restraining ourselves from laying them upon others is the next best thing to removing them: *this is the minimum goal for which any spiritual aspirant should strive.* Joy and happiness can come later, but at least we can resolve to not bring unhappiness to anyone else. That much we owe the world. Of the two kinds of spiritual practitioners – those who practice for themselves and those who practice for the sake of others – this one is a "for the sake of others" practice, which makes it a superior practice.

Since it is very practical, a sort of mind-improvement (*blo-jong*) exercise, it falls within the "method" side of Buddhism. However, in order to succeed it is necessary also to diminish one's sense of self-importance. Having a firm sense of the lack of an inherent reality to the personal identity that one has constructed for oneself contributes to one's willingness to surrender the sort of head-strong self-absorption that often accompanies inflicting our obsessions upon others. Undermining the sense of the reality of our ego identity is a "wisdom" practice, and one really needs to work both sides of the street, method *and* wisdom, if one is going to succeed in keeping one's own negative energies from contaminating others.

Take, for instance, not becoming angry when one is frustrated. This can be a problem for me because I enter the world with enough enthusiasm to quickly become obsessed with my projects and so am unable to suffer hindrances well. I have little patience, and my impatience can lead me to brief fits of explosive energy that damage the mind-stream of others. Even when I am aware of what is happening, I am unable to keep a lid on it, sometimes with unfortunate results.

I remember one occasion in the spring of 1984 when the Ganden Tripa, the highest lama of the Gelugpa order, came to the US to each a great text by Tsong Khapa that I had been trying to study for some time, *The Essence of Well Spoken Explanations* (*Legs bshad snying po*), a text that summarized the views of emptiness of the various schools of Buddhist tenets. I was living in Eugene, Oregon, at the time, and the Ganden Tripa was to give these special teachings in Los Angeles nearly a thousand miles away. Fortunately, the teachings were scheduled for the spring break of my university, and they were to commence on the morning of Saturday following my last lecture (the preceding Thursday), which left me only Friday for the long drive.

I made the journey in my car, stayed with a friend, and showed up barely on time as the Ganden Tripa walked into a suburban home on Los Angeles' Westside a mile from where I grew up. Most of the students sitting on the living room floor looked like me – tanned, fit, jeaned and T-shirted in the understated but affluent Westside way. The truth of suffering was far from our experience or, given our youth, even our understanding. The Ganden Tripa gazed at us with no small amount of wonder, and he could probably sense the lack of discipline in us. He was silent for many minutes as he studied us. I looked about to observe what he was studying and saw at once that we must seem to him people who had taken our privilege for granted, just as residents of the god realms do.

There we sat, the tanned and beautiful people, infatuated with our own beauty. The high lamas may not really be omniscient, but it would have required something less than omniscience to have recognized our self-absorption. In fact, self-absorption may be the social trait that best characterizes the residents of my homeland, Southern California. After some ten minutes the Ganden Tripa announced that he did not think it was suitable to be teaching us Tsong Khapa's *Essence of Eloquent Explanations*, and instead he launched into many days of descriptions of the hell-realms from *The Graduated Path* (*Lam rim*), teachings that I had heard too many times before.

My spring-break was destroyed.

All of my considerable efforts and expense were arranged without result, and I was sorely disappointed. The living room was unable to contain my frustration. As the lecture on the hell realms continued, my frustration grew into anger, leaving me powerless. Perhaps throwing my own ugliness into my face was the teaching that I most needed at that time, I cannot say. But I did recognize at once that I did not have the capacity to control my growing anger at the Ganden Tripa, the throne holder of the Gelug sect of Tibetan Buddhists! I considered the other attendees, locals whose interest in *The Essence of Well Spoken Explanations* was perhaps not as great as mine and who might benefit from the Ganden Tripa's talks. I did not want to disrupt their opportunity by inflicting my afflicted emotions upon them, so I went out to my car and drove back to Eugene that same day, channeling all of my agitated energy into the freeway driving. My dharma gift to my fellow seekers was to remove my sorry ass from the mind-space of that Los Angeles living room filled with young dharma students.

Reflecting on matters as I made the two-day return drive home, I thought it was a good thing to be able to recognize when my energy has lost the capacity to make any contribution. I resolved to become more aware of my energy this way in the future. But resolve by itself is capable of achieving little. All of our good ideas and all of our resolutions to be good have no more effect than a smoker's New Year's resolution. It's a good idea, but not yet an actual practice. Little is to be gained from resolution that is not accompanied by some habituation with the virtuous actions and mind-streams that one aspires to. The energy flows of a smoker have already been fully integrated with his or her life practices, and change can come only with re-*habituation*, not with ideas. Cultivating virtuous energy-streams is a very slow practice, whose results are measured not in weeks but decades. In fact, many Tibetans would say not in decades but in lifetimes.

That is really the great wisdom of the Tibetan method of Buddhist practice. This re-"habituation" is frequently mislabeled as "meditation." "Cultivation" is also a felicitous translation. My friends and I usually reify "meditation" as a sort of add-on Thing, which we can choose to do at certain times and not do at other times. It is even sometimes restricted to a place, but it is really something that happens inside-out, not outside-in, and the practice has more to do with results than with any physical act like sitting. The real point is to re-form *the systems* of energy that flow habitually through one's mental stream (the "mind" here being the heart) so that one no longer has a choice regarding acting with or without virtue – one just does it naturally, habitually.

This is partly why philosophical studies do not always afford a complete means for taming the mind. My Western teachers were brilliant, but many of them were untamed, which drove me to Buddhist practice. One must re-form the autonomic nervous system to be gentle, kind, and caring –

good ideas can help a lot, but they need to be deposited and cultivated in the chakras at one's heart and navel. Take for instance one of my teachers at Sera, Geshe Tenpa Chophel. As he once explained to me, there are five standards of geshe (professor). He used his hand to describe the thumb as the best quality geshe, followed by the index finger, and after the middle and ring fingers he pointed to his little finger and explained that he was the lowest class of geshe. What utterly sincere humility! In his mid-60s he had a stroke and lost much of his memory of the texts, and even some mantras. He even forgot the faces of many of his students, including myself. But he had meditated for so many years and had engaged in taming his mind over many decades, that after his stroke his gentleness, kindness, and concern for others had not abated in the slightest. I compare that to the stroke of one of my uncles, which rendered him easily irritated, even against his wishes. Many of the ideas had vanished in Geshe Tenpa Chophel's mind, but the tamed habituation of his deeper physical energies was still in force after the stroke: he was an accomplished lama, despite his self-assessment. When I visit him I am always overjoyed to witness his enduring achievement, something that I aspire to if all my ideas can stop getting in the way.

My resolve during the drive back in 1984 had little effect upon me at the time, and I continued to burden others with my impatience. Some skill-in-means did begin to show itself 25-years following that resolution, when I came so close to dying that I was afforded an opportunity to let go entirely (see Chapter 44). Since then, there have been some days during which my re-programming is successful. For the numerous times I still fail, I carry a spare book, in order to pull my negative energy out of the environs. I recognize that using a book this way is a thin substitute for patience, but it is effective as skillful means. Just carrying it sometimes reminds me of my commitment.

So *the point of my practice* is this: never mind trying to purify my garbage; just let me prevent it from polluting others' minds. After all, they have enough of their own mental contamination to contend with without adding to their task. That daily aspiration is my minimum responsibility as a human being.

16
Greeting Others

One of my newest friends at Sera Monastery is Tsewang the office assistant, whose job is to tirelessly serve each person who comes to the monastery office. We hit it off well from the very first, since I instantly admired his efficiency and lack of ego. After a number of pleasant interactions, we became sort of casual buddies. After I retreated to my quarters in the monastery's large guesthouse in order to complete a translation of a 17th century Tibetan text, I did not see him for nearly a month.

With the onset of the monsoon I developed an allergy, and the constant nasal dripping it created had kept me up much of the night for several nights in a row, leaving me in an exhausted condition. One day around noon, after my morning session of translating was completed, I went downstairs to the front of the guesthouse to collect my daily newspaper. As I strolled along the upstairs porch, I could see that someone who looked very much like Tsewang had entered the grounds. But after closer inspection I decided that it was someone else, and I thought to myself, "I'm glad it's not my friend, since my head is too clogged for me to interact with anyone."

Being in my mid-60s, my eyesight has grown poor, and I kept looking out to determine whether the figure was he or not. My staring out compelled the figure to look back, but I was unable to make out whether it was really Tsewang. Perhaps the figure saw me looking, or as it approached the front door it offered a wave to someone else it saw inside, or to me – I could not see anything clearly enough to determine which. As the person climbed the steps and entered the building, I once again concluded that it was not Tsewang.

However, as I was heading down the stairs I ran into him coming up the stairs, and then I waved hello: But my mood was not good due to my lack of sleep, my not wishing to interact publicly, and my having already soured the greeting by not returning his previous wave that turned out to have been a greeting for me. Without wanting to, I may have inadvertently signaled a downgrading of our relation, even though my estimation of him had not changed in the slightest. This led me to reflect upon the fine subtleties that accompany our gazes when we greet others. Our daily mundane interactions are filled with these minute and intricate miscommunications, which is why Shantideva's text, *Compendium of Good Advice* (*bsLab pa kun mthus*) spends so much time offering detailed instructions on the mundane aspects of how we walk, gaze, frown, and speak.

Even the best of humans continually assess the esteem in which other people hold them, frequently on the basis of only a look, and it is only the most accomplished yogi who is entirely unconcerned with how other people look at one or the valuation that such looks can bear. As we walk about the streets of the world, there are hundreds of pairs of eyes seeking some self-affirmation, and people scrutinizing this estimation of them that is available in the look of the other. For this reason, if we care about other's feelings, we need to make our own looks affirming ones. Make sure that even casual acquaintances know that we consider them worthy. Genuine fellow feeling is best of course, but even a simulation of good feeling is preferable to a steely coldness. Here the practice amounts to this: we need to deliberately go around *distributing kind gazes* as gifts for the people we pass. Naturally, our friends should be included in this policy.

Lobsang Jinpa, Abbot of Kyil Khang monastery at Tashi Lhunpo in 1850, wrote, "One becomes preoccupied with the way that others look at one, scrutinizing each of those looks for evidence of favor or condemnation; and even a hint of disapproval becomes hard for one to bear."[3] Wouldn't it be nice to have so much harmony within oneself that one was not vulnerable to the judgments of others? One's looking and being looked-at are subtle and deep phenomena. It would be especially great to not let the favor or disfavor that another reveals in his or her look cloud our opinion of *them*! This would be the way of a spiritual warrior. Of course, it is natural for us to feel objectified by the other's look, yet in that objectification we also come to recognize that we do indeed have a responsibility to the one whose eyes are gazing at us. Emmanuel Levinas has advised, "We need to always keep ourselves open to the look of the other." However, cultivating a responsibility for others does not mean we need to depend upon others' constant approval, as if we were hungry ghosts.

In the instance that occurred at the monastery guesthouse, I had not understood with any certainty that someone was greeting me, or that it was someone that I knew. Nevertheless, the next time that I ran into Tsewang, I could not help but observe that our relation had indeed experienced a slight downgrading, a downgrading I did not seek, nor felt our relationship deserved. But my perceived failure to return a greeting had had consequences, however inadvertently. This is an important lesson: relations not only depend upon the genuine feelings one has for the other, *they also depend upon appearances*. That is why we must work at using appearances skillfully, why we have a responsibility to continuously attend to how we look at other people and greet them. In an earlier century this went by the name of courtesy, even honor. When it is fueled by a genuine interest in gladdening the hearts of others, it

---

[3] Lobsang Jinpa [blo bzang sbyin pa], *Relinquishing the Extreme Views Belonging to Common Sense: An Explanation of the Meaning of the Great Mudra's Basis, Path, and Result* (*gzhi lam 'bras bu'i phyag chen gyi don rnam par dshad 'dzin mthar skrod*), nd. p. 37.

can be considered kindness. The best way to ensure that your interest is genuine is to look directly into the eyes of the other person and smile, and then let your gaze linger, demonstrating that you have the time for them – don't simply look away as if your smile was perfunctory but stick with the other person's eyes until you both have acknowledged some kindness in each other. That takes more time than many people have today, but it is an important part of being human.

17
My Thinking Keeps Getting In Its Own Way

One of the debates that has divided the various sects and scholars within Tibetan Buddhism itself has been an argument over to what degree one needs to employ formal analysis in one's practice. There are some sects who are distrustful of too much incessant analysis and believe that while it may be used for solving problems, it produces as many problems as it resolves. Other sects devote two decades to scholarly pursuits, mastering texts, debating epistemology, etc. The former sects argue that one would do better just to meditate quietly and learn how to cut off one's intellection, while the latter sects argue that if one has not properly understood the actual way that phenomena appear, one could not have understood anything worth meditating about and one would simply be acting like a cow in the field. They add that if all that was needed was to keep thoughts from arising, then by this time there would be many cows who are enlightened beings. If one has not learned how the mind causes problems, then stopping the mind only works while the mind is stopped, but as soon as one arises from one's meditation all of the delusions in which one has invested oneself will reappear.

A deep irony works at the heart of all thinking, including formal analysis: *one's thoughts can get in the way of one's thinking*. Buddhists thinkers say that one cannot *formulate* in words what is the direct experience of the emptiness of inherent essences, for the reason that such experience cannot be described and our efforts to do so can themselves become distractions. The first stanza of the *Tao Te Ching* by Lao Tzu, one of the world's oldest books, cautions, "The truth that can be told is not the eternal truth." This indicates (1) that there is truth; and (2) that the truth cannot be captured by efforts to represent it in formal analytic terms. The first great Panchen Lama Losang Chögyi Gyaltsen endorses this insight when he argues that ultimately emptiness is *ineffable*.[4] The difficult thing about things that are ineffable is that it means that any effort to describe matters comprehensively is doomed to failure.

In spite of that, it is well established that practice in Buddhism involves *both* discerning awareness (*vipaśyanā*) and calm abiding (*śamatha*), and one of the techniques of discerning awareness is formal analysis. It is widely concluded that cutting off any and every thought that comes to the mind is preparation for becoming stupid. Does not wisdom *include* studying matters, and then using what one has learned? Thinking that the main challenge is to cut off analytic thinking is foolish, yet I have many friends who think this way. The challenge is to learn how to use analytic thinking. It is for certain that too much intellection can be a problem, even an affliction. Socrates himself claimed at the end of his life that the only thing that he was able to know for sure was that he knew nothing; however, he gained this very insight by analyzing the nature of thinking, not by just sitting silently. As humans, we are condemned to reason. Using reason or not is not a choice for us, since as *Homo sapiens sapiens* it is our destiny to think! Our name itself says, "the hominid that thinks." In

---

[4] *brjod du med* pa, in *bDag 'dzin gshags 'debs dgra dpung brag ri 'joms pa'i gnam lcags 'khor lo 'bar ba* (*The Blazing Wheel of Thunderbolts That Split Asunder the Rocky Mountain of Reifying Habits*), *Collected Works of the Panchen Lama Losang Chögyi Gyaltsen*, p. 374.

fact, we think so much that the word *sapiens* appears twice in our scientific name. Since we are condemned to thinking, we have attempted to organize our thinking as best we can; however, those very ways that we use to keep our thinking organized easily lend themselves to becoming another cause for distraction that obscures what we wish to think most! In short, our thinking keeps getting in our way.

And yet we must think. The Tibetans have a great word to describe the way that thinking keeps running away with itself: *spros pa*, which means "conceptual elaboration," the proliferation of notions that keep cascading off one another. Our thinking flourishes just like the branching of a tree: one limb leads to two branches, and then those limbs have more branches, and soon our thinking runs away with itself. Extensive mental proliferation occurs in the span of an instant, like the speed-up of some time-lapse photography of a sprouting tree. If the momentum of our thinking never pauses, we will be left with a frenzied existence, even when we use the best analytic traditions in the world. Although humanity has evolved a great deal over the 120,000 years of our existence, we have not evolved enough so that we know how to use properly this gift of analytic thinking that we bear, and so we still have much to learn. Since we have existed for so short a time, this is not really surprising. Our real challenge is that we need to evolve further.

The point of employing reason is not so that our formal analyzing can dominate our experience, even though it is easy for this to happen. As Panchen Losang Chögyi Gyaltsen has written, "Clever scholars understand a great many things, but they miss the one!"[5] The problem here may be that those who are the most skilled at analyzing matters formally are the ones most unable to let go of it,

---

[5] *bDag 'dzin gshags 'debs*, p. 313. For an English translation, see *The Panchen Lama's Debate Between Wisdom and the Reifying Habit*, Delhi: Motilal Banarsidass.

and so in the end they can find no peace. Such thinkers resemble my neighbors who live on Rancho El Socorrito in Baja California, Mexico. Mostly American retirees, they arrive here when they are in their 50's and 60's, and they lease some empty property near the beach; but then they must build their retirement home. This work of building, which is necessary, keeps them busily occupied for a couple of years, and during this time they keep each day well organized with their purposes – the building tasks, materials purchasing, painting, plumbing, trimming, etc. – until when their home is finally completed they find themselves at a loss for what to do next! This can lead to an existential crisis. And just like those who think too much, they don't recognize when it is time to stop their calculating. So they build a garage. After the garage, there is a workshop; after that it is a new patio, etc. They are constantly *doing*, and might well die of boredom if they should ever be restricted only to *being*; and yet it is only by learning how *to be* that we really become accomplished human *be*-ings.

Thinking, even by the best philosophers, can be like that. So accustomed do thinkers become to their analytic routines that when these routines have completed the work they were intended to accomplish, they cannot leave them aside and move along; instead, they continue *doing* their analyses. Wittgenstein once said that an analytic tool should be used the way that one uses a ladder: once one has climbed to where one needs to go, one should cast it aside. The Tibetans employ a similar analogy: formal analysis should be used like a raft to get to the other side of a raging river; once one is across, one does not need to keep carrying the raft. How do we learn to use reason when it is required, while also knowing when to be silent, as Socrates suggested? As the Dalai Lama has put the matter, how do we get *reflection* to contribute to a "balance of a tranquil working of the mind" without reflection itself becoming a problem?[6]

On the one hand we cling to words and meanings, reifying their truths and concretizing reality itself, a reality that we ourselves are fabricating with those very ideas. Yet on the other hand there are those practitioners, even some Buddhists, who argue that we need to stop analyzing and cut off our thoughts so we can just "meditate" without thinking or analyzing. If it is true that we have done enough thinking to have wrapped our minds tightly with the threads of our elaborations (the *spros pa*), then we have to actively *undo* those threads; and as if to add to the irony of our situation, that will require some more analyzing of how our thoughts have spun those fabrications that we believe in. Here is a clue: whenever one has come to believe one's own propaganda, that is the time for a bit of analysis!

Normally, when we find ourselves occupied with understanding the world, it is easy to miss the fundamental structure of understanding itself: we project the structure of our ideas upon experience, and that experience conforms with whatever projections we have applied in trying to understand it. Buddhist teachers suggests that in addition to understanding the world, we should also try to understand the nature of understanding. This kind of "reflexive" looking requires us to pull apart our prejudices, our pre-judgments, in what some call an act of de-construction. It is in this sense that wisdom can consist of knowing less just as easily as it can consist of knowing more. In fact, ignorance operates by blindly superimposing its pre-understandings upon the world, leaving no space to learn anything new. The ways that our own thinking contaminates the world, the way our thinking finds itself always already inscribed in the products of thought, which we foolishly imagine to be existing on their own,

---

6 Dalai Lama Tenzin Gyatso *Violence and Compassion,* NY: Doubleday, 1994, p. 84.

independently of our production, are too subtle for us to fully describe here;[7] however, the reason that we cannot abandon rational analysis is that we need to spend years studying the dynamic work of meaning production and developing the capacity to identify thinking that gets in its own way before we cease being our own worst enemy.

That is why many Tibetan monks spend two decades analyzing epistemological problems before they commence serious meditation. When they finally do extended retreats, they have acquired something to meditate upon. As the Tibetologist Matthew Kapstein has said, "This philosophy, in the end, is not primarily about objects of thought, but rather is a way of coming-to-be – one that we are enjoined to bring to fruition within ourselves."[8] How do we learn how to use analytic thinking to find a way of being that itself is the best fruit of our practice? Anne Klein has suggested, "When one is properly trained, analysis *itself* induces a state of calm abiding on emptiness."[9] How do we learn to think with *sukha* (comfort) like that?

Tsong Khapa concludes his extensive *Lam Rim* by commending "the ultimate analysis that examines the mode in which things exist."[10] This "ultimate analysis" stems from the analysis of Nagarjuna, who stated in his *Root Stanzas on the Middle Way*, "Anything that exists as interconnectedly dependent is by its nature already

---

[7] For a detailed account, please see Kenneth Liberman, "The Reflexive Intelligibility of Affairs," *Cahiers Ferdinand de Saussure: Revue suisse de linguistique générale* 64, pp. 73-99.

[8] Matthew Kapstein, *Reason's Traces*, Boston: Wisdom, 2001, pp. 14-15.

[9] Anne Klein, *Path to the Middle*, NY: SUNY Press, 1994, p. 15.

[10] Tsong Khapa, *Byang chub lam rin chen mo* (*The Graduated Path to Enlightenment*), Amdo, China: The Blue Lake People's Publishing House, nd., p. 774.

pacified."[11] The most remarkable thing about Nagarjuna's method of dialectical reflection is that it is capable of undoing each thought as it erects it. It takes up ideas that we have become attached to, massages them, demonstrates their shortcomings and the falsehoods they bear, until we loosen the tight grasp we have of them. In that loosening there is a calm ease or *sukha* that comes about. We can think, but it is without the frenzy or excitation that characterizes many analytic efforts. In this instance, analysis and calm are not opposed – the analysis *itself* is utilized as the vehicle that induces the calm. In this way analysis can establish the *sukha*. It is not the analyzing itself that does the damage to our mode of being in the world, it is *the fastness* of the focusing energy that is sometimes required while analyzing that unhinges us and lets loose the proliferating elaborations that we are then no longer able to control. So the practice here becomes learning how to slow down this use of reason, and to apply it without compulsiveness. As Tsong Khapa insisted, without calm abiding no discerning awareness can be generated.[12] The point is that our attention to "practice" or *sādhana* (Sanskrit) is as important as any analytic insight, for the reason that even though the mind knows that it should stop analyzing (after it has learned what is required for a given situation), it is unable to do so.

While it is true that analysis can become distraction, it does not have to be that way. The key here is that we need to allow the dialectics of our analyses to carry us along with its own flow like a slow river, and we then can apply that pliancy (a fabulous Tibetan notion, *shin byang*, the key to success here) within the analysis itself. Even though most formal analysis does not typically call forth this kind of stabilization of our energy, it has the capacity to do so.

---

[11] Nagarjuna, *dbU ma rtsa ba shes rab*, Chapter 7, Verse 16.
[12] Tsong Khapa, *Byang chub lam rin chen mo*, p. 786.

This is "the radiance of wisdom"[13] referred to in the *Yoga Sutra*. The Panchen Lama refers to this process during his description of how a practitioner develops "an intense lucidity" (*gsal ngar*) that serves as its *own* methodology and becomes the basis for calm reconciliation while it continues its steady work of unraveling the obsessive attachments we have thought up for ourselves. We should not surrender formal thinking! But the medium of reasoned reflection needs to become the basis for its own stabilization. This would entail our abiding in the mood or temporality of the mind that is doing the analyzing, observing the analysis as we are analyzing, which is a form of detachment. Our practice here involves learning to extend this sense of stabilization so that we can think and be detached at the same time, or rather, so that instead of racing to another obsession our thinking itself fosters a stabilized flow, *is* this flow, this *sukha.* Gradually, we can learn to develop a powerful tool that will assist us daily in our life practice without creating more problems than it resolves.

[13] *Jñāna dīptihi*; Patañjali, *Yoga Sutra*, Book 2, Verse 28.

18
The No Honking Challenge

As a native of Los Angeles, I have spent much of my life waiting at red lights. As a teenager in the 1960's, I used to marvel at how many dozens, and hundreds, of red lights I would be caught up with on any given day. How many red lights does it takes to exceed the limits of sanity? Mid-town traffic especially was a major challenge to the hormones of a teenager. Some days I would try to count them in order to see if I could reach a hundred. The red lights of Los Angeles are one of the worst features of the city, disqualifying it from a place where I would reside permanently, despite being a loving native.

The traffic of today renders these red lights of yesteryear the halcyon days. What were then simple two-way lights now are more usually four and five-way traffic flows, and one could write a short poem in the time it takes for a signal to run from one green light to the next. Some of the corners deserve a place in Charlie Chaplin's classic movie, "Modern Times." There are so many cars that operate in these inexorable flows that they have designed most of the newer districts of "The Southland" for the cars only, ignoring the needs of pedestrians. Southern Orange County and Northern San Diego County are great places to live if one is an automobile, but they are no places for pedestrians. It is not the length of the waiting among the intensive flows of sun-reflecting rear windows that is the difficulty, it is the number of times each day that one must do the waiting. Each corner offers its own version of eternity, throughout the Southland. If the 1960s required patience, today one has to be a bodhisattva to arrive at one's destination in a good mood.

If one fights it, one will become a nervous wreck. Like mosquitoes, its nefarious effects upon the nervous system are cumulative. If tantric practice involves the use and control of one's vital energies, by what method can one use self-control to turn this cavalcade of red lights into the path?

It is said that the "Method" half of Tibetan Buddhism (the other half is "Wisdom") rests squarely upon the dual practice of taming one's anger and generating an eagerness to assist each person one meets. The root cause of all our troubles is an untamed mind. In the case of taming anger, the key is a mind-over-matter, psyche-over-body minimization of one's impatience. Can the use of L.A.'s red light signals serve as a basis for practicing patience? It is easy to practice patience when one is relaxing at a remote resort; but it is better when one can practice it amidst the tumult of a crowd. The key is to take responsibility for not generating enmity or anger towards others and instead to generate support and affirmation for each person one encounters. There may be no better cauldron for forging one's patience than the red traffic lights of Los Angeles.

Why *is* there so much rushing around in Los Angeles? A single week there leaves me exhausted. And the traffic is the worst part of it. While L.A. drivers there move more safely than drivers in most other cities, they make abundant use of their horns. Everyone is constantly blasting the horn, not to avoid danger but most commonly as instruments for moral recrimination. And why is it so difficult for people to allow a path for a car that is attempting to merge on the freeway? It is not as if one never enters a freeway oneself. On a recent trip to São Paolo, Brazil, I discovered traffic jams that were the worst I'd ever experienced. One can get locked up in a congested block for an hour or more, block after block, yet no one there honks the horn! To me, that was a radical social event, and in light of that experience I realized for the first time that the continual horn honking that takes place in America (again, related to moral recrimination) or in India (simple self-assertion without moral implications) is a *social* practice and not at all an inevitable component of driving in heavy traffic, as I believed it to be. After I returned to Los Angeles, I decided to take a "No Honking Challenge": I resolved to never honk in L.A., except when it was necessary for avoiding a collision. What I discovered is that my day's driving produced considerably less stress.

During one of those days I was late, in this case while arriving at the home of my cousin, who lived in a project of houses that has as more cul-de-sacs than throughways. Not wanting to arrive too late for dinner, I became anxious, when I came upon two cars that were stopped in the middle of the road, impeding my passage. I deduced at once that the person in one of the cars was explaining some directions to the person in the other car. Recalling my No Honking Challenge, and that I myself often halt to ask for directions, I sat and waited patiently. I observed that the two of them were being friendly and considerate, so I celebrated them instead of pressing them out of their social harmony by insisting upon my priority. Practical Buddhism consists of events this small, but they quickly add up. Yet many people run around the city subsuming others under their own agendas. It may be that the way that driving automobiles individualizes public life has set people into continuously competitive relations, and I have often wondered whether one benefit of public transport might be to foster more sociality than can occur when a single person in each car has to vie with other "individuals" for increasingly scarce road space. On the other hand, one can use challenging situations like these for learning how to practice generosity and overcoming competitiveness.

The average American might think, "Why on earth would I wish to surrender any advantage?" But I have a close Indian friend, now living in Portland, who spent a decade as a rickshaw driver in India (he was my rickshaw driver in Mysore during the 1990s), and who informed me recently, "Rickshaw driving taught me many great things! It taught me tolerance. It taught me about people. It taught me patience. Rickshaw driving gave me everything, especially contentment; and you cannot discover that easily." So it *is* possible to turn any adverse circumstance into an occasion for practice.

One can learn a good deal by looking for how people practice patience in heavy traffic, and one can learn even more by being patient oneself. Once while I was riding a full bus in Santos, Brazil, a potential passenger arrived at the bus a mere second after the driver had closed the doors. Many bus drivers would have opened the door, for he had not yet begun his departure. The potential passenger pleaded with the driver to let him on, raising his index finger as if to say, "Just one more person cannot do any harm." But the driver was eager to be on his way and put his foot on the gas pedal. Instead of being angry, the supplicant waved his hand in a sweet farewell that indicated, "Alright, I understand. Have a nice day." He was not angry. I wonder how many people throughout the world would have shouted an epithet or raised a fist at one who contravened their self-interests that way. It is common enough in Los Angeles that is for sure. This Brazilian was admirable. I hope to emulate him one day, when my Buddhist practice improves.

It is said that when another becomes angry with us or shows disrespect, one should accept that person as one's teacher of patience and be grateful for the opportunity to be exposed to one's own impatience. The red lights of the world are excellent teachers of patience, and not relying upon one's horn to relieve that impatience is a good way to start practicing patience. After some time practicing not honking, one can progress to cultivating a bit of gratitude for each red light because it offers one additional opportunity to generate a bout of calm.

There is no true coming or going anyway, and we only travel in circles. In the right perspective, there are no delays.

19
Putting Off Until Tomorrow What One Can Do Today

Optimizing our potential does not always mean to perform more, or to be more active. We fill our lives up daily with activities. Some of these activities are able to calm us – yoga would be one example, reading a good book another, and being with a good friend is a third. Other activities can speed us up, quickening our mental energies and stirring up our adrenal juices. Either kind of activity may be desirable at different times, and the skill-in-means involves knowing which activity is best to engage in on any particular occasion. Our mundane lives consist of exercising this skill-in-means on a continuous basis.

In contemporary society optimizing a situation frequently demands becoming *more* active, even when our physical and spiritual health may benefit more by our being less active. Our body requires some calm in order for the immune response to function well. If we are always tense, the adrenaline will flow, which brings us additional energy at the expense of our immune system. Those times when the body functions primarily in its autonomic nervous system are when the immune response can be most fully activated, such as during sleep, meditation, or during relaxing activities. Each day our body has different needs, and we should develop some body wisdom to recognize those needs, which can even change during the course of a day. To mindlessly keep "doing" may be to exercise more brute ignorance than skill-in-means. That is one of the important lessons yoga can teach.

One thing I find too activating is working at a computer terminal late at night, especially when there are bugs in the software that require solution. At most times I accept computer obstinacy as a cerebral challenge, like any good puzzle. Getting printers to function smoothly, downloading the right driver, sorting out a malfunctioning iPod, getting wireless connectivity to function, or whatever it might be, are inevitable parts of living with computers. There is nothing wrong with such activities in themselves, but when one wishes to calm down from a busy day and prepare for a night of restful sleep, it may be best to leave such puzzle solving and screen-gazing for the next day. We are inviting trouble when prior to our sleep we get our nervous systems stressed by undertaking frenzied tasks as part of our daily productive work, so that the nervous system will keep on running at the same level of speed past the time for it to quit, and we become unable to slow it down.

Moderating the level of our nervous activity is nothing like turning a light switch on and off. Our level of nervous activity has its own momentum, and it requires some time to slow it down by gradually habituating it to progressively slower tasks. Even though we may have 90 minutes available for computer hacking before we have to go to bed, for example, it may be that we will find ourselves unable to "shut down" our own bio-computer as easily as we can our terminal. If that is the situation, then it behooves us to spend that 90 minutes finding a more relaxing activity in order to commence the process of lowering the level of stress in preparation for a night's sleep. Stargazing or book-reading will produce better results.

I have also forbidden myself to use a computer during the first hour after awakening. The opportunity to work quietly in the morning sunlight, with a single-minded concentration focused peacefully upon something profound (which can vary among writing, meditation, and reading the most challenging text currently resting on my desk) is too precious to surrender to the Red Bull-like jolt that connecting with the internet can give. While the internet promises to deliver the world, too frequently it delivers superficialities that masquerade as important. So I delay it for that first, most productive hour.

It is good to offer our body calm at the beginning and conclusion each day. On occasion the body will be exhausted from too much physical labor, or one can feel run down just by successfully fighting off a cold – the body has its own ways. The ability required may consist of simply recognizing accurately what the body needs and not forcing ourselves beyond our optimal capabilities. There are always contradictions too, since sometimes we may be able to enhance our natural capacity by pushing ourselves a little bit past the point at wish we wish to stop; but the key words here are "a little bit," which is something quite different from "on and on." The critical mistake is being unable to recognize the "on and on" before it occurs. That "on and on" can eventually lead to madness. We must learn to act wisely.

Yesterday was a day of endless activities, all congenial to me: I surfed for two hours, read forty pages from a challenging text on Buddhist epistemology, wrote some letters on the computer, sent some emails via my satellite internet hookup, jogged two miles, and then commenced my 75 minute-long Ashtanga yoga practice on my roof. My body was tired, not so much from the active day as from a series of active days, and I realized that it was time to rest. Midway through my *āsana* practice, I fell into some deep relaxation in between each position, and so I cultivated them. My nerves seemed to bathe in the conscious relaxation I was able to find while dwelling in between each one. The day's yoga asana practice resided not in the actual positions themselves but in the resting between them, so that the resting periods took three times longer than the actual position-taking. I was amazed at how peaceful I felt there up on my roof, looking at the ever-blue Baja sky. Finally, I suspended my practice half-way through and just relaxed, in what recent yogis call *yoga nidraa*. But the name is probably more of a distraction than an aid – it is simply surrendering to some rest when your body is seeking it.

After my practice I came downstairs and cooked dinner, and I had planned to solve my printing problems (two computers and two printers, with none of them functioning together). I knew it would be a "busy" activity if I was to have any success at it. My judgment was that I should not be re-stirring my nervous system after it had finally settled itself into a sweet purr, and I feared that any new busy-ness might intervene with a good night's sleep. So I abandoned the last of my "day's chores," and started a Western novel by Larry McMurtry. I read for 90 minutes, and then dropped into nine full hours of recuperative sleep, arising early to take up my agenda again the next day.

III

Tales From Around the World

20
The Goat (La Capra)

Maria is 85 years of age. Her husband, my mother's first cousin, died 35 years previously, in our centuries-old family home near Naples, the very home in which my grandmother was born and where Maria still lives after raising her two children there. Since her children are now adults (not far from retirement themselves) she has been living alone. Each morning upon arising, Maria begins her day by watering several dozen plants that grow in pots on her balcony. During this half-hour daily ritual, Maria caresses each plant. More than friends, she offers them adoring love, and she claims that they console her greatly. Plants indeed can do this, but that depends very much upon *one's own capacity* for loving. It is another example of how one's capacity to love others will result in some affection in return.

Maria also knits, and what she knits is never something that is for her. She knits for her grandchildren or for the grandchildren of friends. How many centuries of altruism have been knitted into garments made by grandmothers over all the ages? Who needs prayer or meditation when there exist such practices that we can use for cultivating fond regard for others, stitch by stitch? The last time I saw her knitting it was a covering for a table in the family crypt, so her love extends to those who have passed on, including her husband. Each stroke, each half-stitch, is for Maria an effective practice of loving kindness.

When I first met Maria four years previously, she was anticipating her open-heart surgery and was anxious about it. Having already undergone open-heart surgery myself, I offered her the best counsel I could, explaining that it was likely to the point of certainty that she would survive but that it would be extremely painful. When I saw her during my subsequent visit, I asked her about her surgery before discussing anything else. Maria was impressed that I had cared enough to remember it and also to ask about it so immediately. But consider which is the greater indication of kindness: concern for another's health *or* concern that is able to admire the concern that someone may have for another person's health? The capacity for being moved deeply by a small act of kindness can exceed the compassion of that small act of kindness itself.

Again, when I had returned to the ancestral home after a week of visiting southern Italy, Maria informed me that another of my mother's cousins, who lived in an even more ancient house across the street, had gone away for a week of summer holiday and so had all her nephews who lived there. She said that the other house (constructed by our family in 1150) was entirely empty at the moment. I asked her who was feeding the goat. At this, Maria exclaimed to her daughter, "Listen to this! He is so focused upon everyone's needs that he shows concern even for the goat!" The honest truth is that I asked only out of the abstract curiosity of a sociologist who is interested in local cultural practices, with barely a shred of thought for the goat. Too bad for me! The one with the compassion, including compassion for the goat, was Maria, not I. Her thoughts tended naturally toward others' welfare and in this case it included the welfare of the goat. It was the case that Maria's goodness had so much vitality that she kept projecting that goodness upon others, even when it was lacking.

How do I explain to her that my goodness is a figment of her imagination, a result of her own goodness, which exceeds mine. I could try to explain across the gulf of my inadequate Italian and her benevolent ways that the selflessness of a compassionate observer, like those who see beauty, resides in the heart of the one who beholds. Instead, I silently study her benevolence, and celebrate it.

Such *celebration* is an effective dharma practice much emphasized by Buddhists. It is almost as good for the practitioner as compassion. Although celebrating selflessness is not as good as selflessness itself, it encourages progress in that direction. It took Maria 85 years to perfect her level of benevolence, and it would require a great deal of study to determine everything she did to achieve it. I decided that it was probably better for her if I did not undermine her confidence in other people's good will by reversing her positive notions about me.

21
The Pride of Overcoming Pride

There is a respected family in Calcutta who proudly trace their family line back to Advaitacharya, a Vedanta saint renowned for his having overcome the ego and who distinguished himself by his contributions to philosophical theory and also by his personal practice. His fame was so great that even now, some four centuries later, this family proudly preserves his memory. The children of the family take up their spiritual responsibilities with an air of confident authority: they have enshrined egolessness itself and have even made it the focus of their self-esteem.

Today the curse that this great saint of ego-destruction cast upon his family and progeny is to heighten their sense of ego-attachment, almost in perpetuity! They practice the pride of having overcome pride. If Advaitacharya had been able to see the effect that he has had upon generations of his family line, he might have opted for selfishness.

I am able to recognize this situation readily, without having to make much effort, since I have observed my own pride about overcoming ego. I have been able to examine this pride recurrently because it arises in me so much of the time. I haven't managed to overcome either my ego or my pride about overcoming my ego, but I *have* managed to do a lot of examination of this flaw of the pride of overcoming pride, and such examination may also be part of the path. Pride is a flaw I share with many of my fellow professors, and that is probably because most professors are not paid as much as people with similar training and capacity, so we make up for it by convincing ourselves that we are somehow better than others. I am reminded of the line from Dylan Thomas' most famous poem that runs, "Though wise men at their end know dark is right/ Because their words had forked no lightning they/ Do not go gentle into that good night."

One professor not like that is my colleague from Italy, Giolo, who was chosen the Assistant Dean of the Faculty of Sociology at Italy's largest, first and best sociology school, which has some 60 faculty. Despite the fact it is a significant honor, more than a year went by before he mentioned it to me, quite accidentally. If I had been made Assistant Head of *anything*, including the smallest, least significant sociology faculty in America, I would have worn the title on my lapel like a badge at a conference, and I would probably seek out conferences to attend only for further opportunities to display that badge.

22
Fearing Anonymity

The first time I met Pastor Ken I was on foot with a surfboard under my arm, walking to the beach. Ken and his wife had just moved in to an older home they purchased in our settlement of retired gringos in Baja California, Mexico, making him my newest neighbor. One of several reasons I like to walk instead of drive the 300 yards to the beach, as my surfing neighbors do, is so that I can interact with people. I also enjoy the feel of the fine sand on the bottoms of my feet, and I look forward to that warm massage on my soles.

Ken was an evangelical minister who had a ministry for his protestant denomination in Baja. Since Mexico is a Catholic country this puts him in a situation of being a member of a minority faith. Perhaps he was feeling a bit of stigma, but when we introduced ourselves, Ken was almost apologetic for his profession. He said to me straight away, "This may sound like a strange thing for a minister to say, but I do not really believe in religion – I believe in God." I replied at once, "That's funny, I'm just the opposite: I don't believe in God, but I do believe in religion. As a sociologist I appreciate the influence that religious institutions can have upon reducing the obsessive attachment of people to distracting materialism and selfishness."

There was a moment of silence, as we both smiled. We were about the same age, both from Southern California, both jocks in our youth, and both very curious men who were fascinated with people. I was able to recognize his good nature right away. I bid him welcome and continued on to my morning of surfing.

Now we greet each other several mornings a week. Mostly we talk about the weather and our joy for living in a place of such quiet beauty. Ken is my kind of minister – he never proselytizes, but he will stick up for his own faith when that is required; of course, he is ready to give religious advice if asked for it. It is missionaries who give spiritual advice when they are *not* asked that I avoid. It is strictly forbidden in Tibetan Buddhism to give any formal instruction unless it is specifically requested. Some missionaries are motivated less by helping people in need than they are by a need to have their own beliefs confirmed, something they accomplish by preaching endlessly. Ken is not that sort. One can also intuit that he has won some major battles on his way to taming his own heart, and I consider any person who has managed to tame his or her heart to be my teacher.

> The steed called mind roams space,
> covering one hundred thousand miles
> in the blink of an eye,
> He who does not know how to tether it
> is apt to be battered to death
> by the inbreath and the outbreath.
>
> Lalla (13th c.)

Ken is also a humble man in most respects, important for a man of God, and he seems uninterested in either becoming rich or in dominating others. As a protestant, he works with the poorest of Mexicans, since more affluent Mexicans work hand-in-hand with the Catholic clergy (a situation not unlike India, where Christianity finds ready converts among the untouchable castes). So I respect Ken's work. While I really know little about his motives, I know a good man when I meet one.

Last week we had the heaviest rains in 17 years, quite literally a gully-washer. It set the wide, dry arroyos to bank-to-bank flooding and transformed the look of the land. So naturally we talked about that during our greeting on my walk back to my house following the morning surf session.

Ken was working near his patio, so I walked over there, surfboard still in arm, and peaked in. I mentioned how I used to do yoga on his patio tile, when the house was unoccupied before he purchased it, since its wall offered some protection from the wind; Ken spoke of how much he and his family love the patio. I then mentioned to him that the site – before the house or patio – is viewable in the old photo album kept by the Mexican family that owns the ranch. Several photos from 50 years before reveal the first gringos to live against our sand dune, probably the first humans to do so since the original Cochimí inhabitants vacated the area more than 200 years ago. I mentioned that the people and houses were different 50 years ago, and that every single one of those gringos has passed away.

"The amazing thing about those photos," I explained, "is that the gringos in the pictures are all the age that you and I are now. They look every bit as confident about their lives as we are; they have a look that seems to suggest that they think they might endure forever." Ken laughed. Encouraged by the laughter, I continued, "You should examine those photos, they are a real teaching. Every person in those pictures is already *completely forgotten*, along with their names, just as we will soon be forgotten. And all this will happen very soon."

Ken's look suddenly grew serious. "No. Speaking for myself, I know someone who will always know me," and he pointed to the sky.

I immediately had two thoughts. First, I observed once again how Europeans always point *up* to the sacred; whereas, the Aboriginal people in Australia I lived with, who were extremely spiritual and related closely to the land via their skin as much as their minds, always pointed *down* to the earth when they waxed spiritual, since they considered *that* to be the holy direction. I reflected about how culturally contingent such gestures were; however, I didn't consider that an observation about this would be useful for the present conversation.

My second thought was that, yes, there may be some argument here. Was he afraid of living without an "I"? I was not suggesting that our being forgotten would create a problem for us, nor was I was suggesting that only a comprehensive and all-denying negation characterizes being. I too feel a strong connection with all of existence, the being that *has always been* and can never be absent, of which I am a part of (though not as an "I" in the way that European metaphysics has hypostatized and reified human identity). I considered conveying this thought to Ken too, that the connections and the at-home-ness we both are able to feel daily might be similar. I also wanted to say that our words are more powerless in all this than he may think. But I considered that he probably considers words to be all-powerful (given how the three Semitic religions have deified the Word), so I decided to pass on this topic too. So we returned to the weather, expressing our wish that we both take full advantage of the splendid post-storm, clear-skied, sunny day, and I continued without delay to my surfing session.

But I felt that I left hanging so much that was important. All of these words about faith, Buddhist or Christian, are vanities. To believe that words can capture the fullness of being, that was the sort of naiveté that those folks in the 50-year old photos displayed. The lesson in humility from considering for a moment the brevity of our reality, a lesson I gain each time I view those photos, was lost, for the reason that Ken would be unable to surrender the individualism that is inscribed in the consciousness of those who practice the Semitic religions. While the individualism of Judeo-Christian civilization affords advantages (like a concern for human rights and civil liberties), it risks encouraging egoism.

My life as a Buddhist began in 1970, when Lama Thubten Yeshe, explaining how to transcend ego-grasping in Christchurch, New Zealand, launched a rocket in my heart. While those who believe in a "soul" can have low egos, it bears dangers despite being without any philosophical grounds. It would have been scandalous, perhaps blasphemy, for me to suggest to Ken that "I" and my "soul" would not be capable of enduring for eternity. I was even thinking that this "enduring" itself, as it is conceived, is far more brief than the eternity with which I do my best to remain connected, and that I would have liked to share with Ken as our common intuitive being. Nor can these words here really convey what I mean, since such experience operates on a level prior to words. The next day I passed Ken's house with only a friendly wave, without further erudition.

Why is there fear of anonymity? The Aboriginal people I lived with in Australia wanted nothing more in life than to keep reclaiming their anonymity, on a daily basis. Ken doesn't realize how strongly he may be holding on to an ego, and he finds fearful the thought that it is inevitable that we will have to surrender up our individual identities.

> I met a traveler from an antique land
> Who said: Two vast and trunkless legs of stone
> Stand in the desert. Near them, on the sand,
> Half sunk, a shattered visage lies, whose frown,
> And wrinkled lip, and sneer of cold command,
> Tell that its sculptor well those passions read
> Which yet survive, stamped on these lifeless things,
> The hand that mocked them, and the heart that fed;
> And on the pedestal these words appear:
> "My name is Ozymandias, king of kings:
> Look upon my works, ye Mighty, and despair!"
> Nothing beside remains. Round the decay
> Of that colossal wreck, boundless and bare
> The lone and level sands stretch far away.
>
> Percy Bysshe Shelley

Grave-markers are another conceit, one that I will avoid. They too involve much belief in words, especially our own propaganda.

For me the heavens and earth resonate in confirmation of being, just as they do for Ken. But there may be no way we can bridge the gulf of words and concepts that abides between our two visions.

23
The Venerable Ani-la

The first time I met the Venerable Ani-la was at the Guest House of Sera Je Monastery, in Mysore District, South India. Both of us had separately gone up to the roof of the Guest House after a several hours-long teaching by His Holiness the Dalai Lama, on Khedrup-Je's *sTong 'Thun Chen Mo*, an encyclopedia of reflections about the nature of emptiness. Much of Tibetan life takes place on their rooftops. That is true for Tibetans who live in the Himalayan mountains, and it is true for them in their adopted homeland in southern Karnataka State. There is something about rooftops that helps to clear out any cobwebs that may form inside of any brain that has been wound too tightly inside of its own cerebrations; and following some six hours of lecture, the cobwebs had formed.

Being a nun, the Ani-la was dressed in her maroon robes, while I was dressed in my Sera *de rigeur* maroon jeans and t-shirt. After several minutes of quiet contemplation, independently of each other, she approached me with some friendly conversation. She had recognized me from other teachings in Dharamsala and Bodh Gaya and had even once attended a talk that I had given at a conference on tantra. We spoke of casual matters (we were engaging in what Tibetans call *cha cho*, i.e. "chit-chat"), including the reasons why I chose to stay at the Guest House instead of in one of the monastic colleges, a choice I made because it placed no constrains upon which Tibetan lamas I could approach for instruction. From there the conversation moved on to her need for funds.

Western *sangha* (clergy) who lack financial support have a difficult time in India. Their customary needs are usually more extensive than those of Tibetan nuns and monks, yet their support network in India is smaller. Moreover, they do not have as many opportunities for financial compensation as do lay Westerners; hence, it is natural for them to approach fellow Westerners when they are in need of money. Life in India can be difficult for anyone without resources, mostly because there is not a good deal in the way of excess resources floating around, in the way there frequently is in European countries and in North America. I could appreciate her predicament, but since I had only just then met this nun, I declined the opportunity.

Over nearly forty years of being a practicing Buddhist in the Tibetan Mahayana tradition, I have known many Western monks and nuns. There have been great souls who were already nuns or monks when I met the dharma, and others who donned robes shortly after that; many among them are still serious practitioners as Buddhist clergy. There were other Western monks and nuns who had given up their robes long ago, yet who have remained quite steadfast on the path of dharma. I have also known laypersons whose practice was exemplary. Further, I have known the most pious monks surrender their robes in order to marry and the most unruly married people decades later take ordination and live model lives. When everything is fully considered, I have not noticed major differences in the perceivable quality of Buddhist practice by Western laypersons and clergy.

To my untutored gaze, there have been a few *sangha* who appeared to me as poor practitioners from the outset, possibly even foolhardy. Oddly, these too have retained or relinquished their robes in about equal numbers. Laypersons seem able to succeed or fail in achieving their best intentions at approximately the rate as *sangha*. I don't give it much thought, and I try to restrict my attention to my own feeble practice (which after four decades has not grown very far beyond the elementary stages). Although since donning robes makes something of a public event out of one's spiritual aspiration, it certainly indicates a special degree of dedication and marks the person as someone one might wish to keep an eye upon, with the idea that something might be learned from their diligent efforts. The advice from sutra that one should not presume that anyone is not a Buddha is pertinent to these considerations, since it fosters a generosity in one's judgments and reminds one that frequently one's judgments are unreliable. It is best not to judge another person, if one is able to desist from doing so.

However, on this noble rooftop at Sera Monastery, the venerable Ani-la would not let the matter of a financial donation rest, even with my refusal, but proceeded to lecture me about how it was the responsibility of laypersons to support *sangha* since the merit to be gained by the practice of *sangha* would benefit everyone's spiritual progress. Although I recognized that it was part of a nun's job description to beg for a living, this Ani-la was unaware that the quickest way to lose the sympathy of an American male was to lecture him about what were his proper responsibilities, so I closed the conversation and retreated to my room downstairs.

Since then, this venerable nun has reappeared at many dozens of dharma teachings and public initiations that I have attended during the last two decades. She always seems to be penniless and displays a remarkable penchant for locating free hand-outs. As far as I am concerned, she is welcomed to them. I have observed her at work locating a likely benefactor, befriending them, and making her requests. She has legitimate needs. She is often sickly and seems to have no means of support, yet she somehow manages to turn up at vital teachings in every corner of the globe, including Mongolia. And she always turns up in the same mood, one of besiegement by a plethora of difficulties, including various systemic health problems (prompting a need for costly herbal remedies from European, Chinese, Ayurvedic and Tibetan traditions, which she carries with her in a heavy bag). But it may be said on her behalf that she certainly has demonstrated a remarkable consistency of right effort in attempting to absorb the teachings of the Mahayana path.

Being a member of the *sangha*, she is entitled to sit up near the front of any teaching, and so it is difficult to refrain from observing her, especially since she is usually quite active in her seat, and her seat is usually in the line of sight between the lay audience and the presiding teacher. During lectures she applies eye drops to her ailing eyes, tiger balm to her sore neck, and fixes a waist strap to her sore back. She carries large bags to hold these aids and medicines, which occasionally spill out onto the cushions, and one cannot help but notice her frequent searches for items amidst all of her pillows.

Suffering from some arthritic pain, some days she finds sitting cross-legged (the de facto position at teachings) difficult, so she fidgets a good deal, moving as many as seven pillows around in a continual search for the optimal arrangement. The pillows are placed and then moved from her backside to her knees, and then to her rear again. The effect of all this is distracting to others, although she herself displays a genuine interest in the teachings. Occasionally, her pillows are piled up so high that if her buttocks miss the top of them as she sits, she will fall over and hit the ground. Some of her fellow *sangha* roll their eyes knowingly at each other at the inevitability of her fussing, but the best practice here lies in not cultivating the slightest feeling of superiority, since doing so would only harm us.

Every teaching it is the same: her mood starts out poor and grows worse as the teachings progress and the sitting becomes more difficult for her arthritis. Her efforts seem concentrated upon colonizing small bits of space at the expense of her neighbors, and those in the know try to choose a seat distant from her. I decided long ago that I would just observe her and not express criticism to others, unless she approaches me personally regarding one or another issue about which she will insist I concern myself. Such people are the real teachers: they push one's weaknesses, they try one's patience, thereby exposing our flaws. One uses such people unwisely when one simply makes them a basis for convincing oneself that one is more advanced.

One is not more advanced – one is *just the same*. I have my own pillow strategies. I keep my books in a special order, along with colored pens and notebooks and dictionaries, all arranged with a special fetish. I have my secret throat drops to reawaken any flagging attention, just as she has. And I also have knees, and so by the end of many weeks of teachings I too am fidgeting about for some relief of the pain in my joints. And I also have devised my own ways to use briefcases and boxes to offer a serviceable surface for my scholarly work. Nearly all of us fuss our way through our lives. No sooner do we become accustomed to a situation that we try to organize it to its "optimum potential" and begin to fuss about the smallest details. Our *own* fussing is what is endless! And that is the truth of it. So I observe her antics in order to learn how to better identify my own.

By the end of the first week of any teaching, all those near her become fed up with her, which strikes me as no way for them to practice dharma. A better practice would consist of *not* getting fed up with her. That is a very real and practical sort of practice. Let me illustrate.

On one occasion the lecture went on for longer than the usual couple of hours. Moreover, the day was quite hot, and it became difficult to concentrate. At one point the venerable Ani-la suddenly hopped up in order to move to a chair, but when she did so her entire apparatus – pillows and small tables piled upon one another like parts of an erector set, with many pens and pencils in a precarious balance – collapsed with a loud slam. It woke quite a few people up, and there was merit in that, but the person next to me leaned over in order to offer me some sarcasm. But I wasn't buying it. My neighbor then rolled his eyes, in a final effort to elicit some sympathetic derision from me; so I leaned over and whispered into his ear, "It is just an allegory for what each one of us is doing, only to a lesser degree."

The next morning my neighbor approached me to thank me for that "instruction." He said he had given my comment some thought and decided that I was right about the matter. I replied that this is what the venerable Ani-la does; her contribution is to teach us about ourselves. And by doing so, she was fulfilling her responsibility well as a member of the clergy. All that was required on our part is a willingness to learn.

24
My Father's "Failure"

At the end of his life, just six months before he died quietly at age 83, shivering one hot summer afternoon with his heater set to high, my father confessed to me that he considered his life to be a failure. He was forced to weep after making this difficult confession to me, the only time I ever saw him cry,

I asked him to explain to me his reasoning for reaching such a conclusion. He replied that he was unable to succeed with either his family or his business. He explained that neither of his two marriages was successful. His marriage to my mother ended when my mother committed suicide after he walked out on her to take up residence with his mistress, who was only six years older than me (he had been carrying on a secret relationship with her for eleven years, a relation I had not known about when I was a teenager). He ended up marrying this mistress, who spent the succeeding two decades spending all of the money generated by the sale of our family's home in Beverly Hills and the insurance money from my mother's suicide (my parents had been married 35 years, so the policy's limitation on suicide had expired). After his money ran out and he had grown old enough to begin receiving social security, the mistress left him.

He lived alone and spent his time mostly contemplating his misdeeds. There was virtue in that. He spent the final decade of his life pining for my mother, and there is no doubt that in the end he suffered from his actions more than she had. In his final years, he came to accept full responsibility for what he did, and this was the only time I felt genuine pride about him.

I expressed to him my opinion that the contrition that he had developed, and for which I was (at last) able to offer him heart-felt respect, was not an inconsiderable accomplishment. I suggested that it was not meant that people should suffer for their misdeeds endlessly, and that he would do better to find some other, more virtuous thoughts to cultivate. He rejected my analysis, saying, "No, I completely blew it in everything I tried to accomplish."

I argued the point, telling him, "Well, I take a slightly different view of success and failure than you do." I asked him, "What do you think the purpose of life is?" He did not have a ready answer. I shared with him the philosophy of my longtime yoga teacher from India, Dr. Swami Gitananda, who once told me, "The purpose of life is to evolve."

"What do you mean?" he asked me.

"It's like this. The way I see it, you were a better person than your father."

"Well, that much is true." His father was an inveterate gambler, and during his lifetime managed to gamble away both his business and two homes; he eventually abandoned his wife and three children, leaving them on the sidewalk. I remember Yonkel well, for his love for me was always genuine and deep. I knew my grandfather only during his last two decades, during which he lived quite amicably with his second wife. They got along extremely well for the reason that both of them were addicted to gambling. At the start of each month when their social security checks arrived, they paid the rent on their apartment (they lived in a mostly run-down section of Los Angeles, now doing better as Koreatown), purchased some food, and then went off to Gardena with what was left of their money to spend a few days playing poker, which had long been legal there. How many days they could keep making the trip depended upon their luck. After they lost what was left, they returned to their apartment to live out the rest of each month.

They even cultivated some discipline in *not* borrowing any money, for the reason that they did not want to use up any money from a succeeding month, which they always reserved for their monthly trip to Gardena. My father knew that by month's end they were always in need, so he would stop by to see them at that time and give them a hundred dollars or so.

My grandfather's death was surely some karmic ripening: he had gone to Gardena at the start of the month (September) as per usual, but this time he had drawn from the deck a royal flush, one of the best possible hands in poker. After decades of gambling failures, at last his ship had come in! He had a massive heart attack on the spot, with his royal flush still in his hands.

He awoke in his hospital bed three days later, while I was sitting there beside him. He looked at me questioningly. I explained to him that he had had a heart attack and had been unconscious for three days. I told him that that very night was Rosh Hashanah, the Jewish New Year's, and he was incredulous; he set his head back down on the pillow to contemplate his situation. After a minute he turned toward me again and asked with some difficulty how he had managed to piss and defecate during the three days. I gestured to the medical apparatuses that were connected to him and explained that they were able to take care of those needs. He flung his hands into the air in the classical ironic Jewish gesture of accepting one's fate, turned his head to the side and fell asleep, a sleep from which he did not again awaken.

My father and his brothers had explained to me the times when they had to sneak out of their Los Angeles apartment windows during the Depression years, in order to escape a landlord who Yonkel was unable to pay due to his gambling losses. In fact, when my father was 13 and for many years thereafter, my father himself raised the money for his family's rent and groceries by going door-to-door fixing radios and other electronic devices in exchange for small donations. By comparison to his father, my father always provided his family with all of the food, clothing, and housing they required, and then some – after all, for most of our years we lived in Beverly Hills. That is why I told him that he had been an improvement upon his father.

I continued. "And please excuse me for the immodesty of this claim, but I think that I am a better person than you are." I did not explain, being somewhat embarrassed, but he understood that I was referring to his cocaine habit, occasional alcoholism, and his infidelity. (I have never taken part in any of those.) I had once joked with him that we could earn a million dollars by making a documentary film of the typical octogenarian cocaine addict in Los Angeles, filming his efforts as he walked with his cane along the street to locate his usual contact, but I didn't bring this topic up then.

"Yes, yes. I agree with that," he told me, relieving me of my embarrassment.

"And I know for certain that my son is a better person than I am." This was true as well. For some reason, my son has inherited few of the neuroses of either of his parents while managing to inherit most of our good qualities, and this has made him an admirable person.

"I know the reason for that," my Dad proffered. "That's because he had a better father than you had."

I found his comment touching, since I knew how hard it must have been for him to say it, and I got a bit choked myself. But I continued, "So if you examine the entire pattern, you can conclude that the history of the entire family through the four generations – from your father, to you, to me, and to my son – is a history in which each generation improved upon the previous one in terms of their personal character. This means that as a family we have managed to *evolve*. So that means that we are a success! You cannot ask for more from life than this."

A moment of silence ensued while he considered my reasoning. Finally he replied, "I like the way you put it," and our tears turned into laughter.

Since I had accomplished my intention of improving his mood, I left the discussion there. But in the years since I have considered carefully the second half of what he called his "failure" in life, his failure in business. His faulty thinking here is a terrific example of how the ordinary way that we think about things is deeply flawed: we objectify a few ideas that get concretized in our thinking and then turn them into absolute truths. By the end, we accept as gospel our own conceptual fabrications. Here is his story.

Having taught himself about electronics, he took a job in the mid 1930s with Los Angeles's foremost radio and phonograph player company. He invented an item that was patented, one of the first automatic record changers, back in the day when most records were 78 rpm. He then ran juke-boxes all over Los Angeles, earned enough to open his own radio and television store, and used the profits there to build and operate a small factory that manufactured television picture tubes in the early days of television (1952). He sold them to the major television companies (RCA, Zenith, Magnavox, etc.), and made a good deal of money doing so; consequently, as a family we moved from being lower middle class to the upper middle class in Beverly Hills. Moreover, he had acquired a swagger, which he was to retain for much of his life. Like many of his era, in his own mind my father thought he was Frank Sinatra.

At this point international economics played a crucial role, even though my father was entirely blind to it, being focused upon only what was closest to his vision. For a full decade Japanese manufacturers of television deliberately sold their sets on the US market for $100 less than it cost them to make and ship them. By 1960, there were few American television manufacturers left – in the end (even today), there were none. His buyers were forced out of business, and the demand for his television picture tubes dried up. He was forced into bankruptcy. This was the great tragedy of his life, for the reasons that (1) he had invested his self-identity egotistically in the notion that he was a self-made wealthy man, and he believed that this essence of his identity was inherent to him; and (2) when his business went bankrupt that had the additional significance, for him at least, that he was bankrupt as a human being.

May we never forget to have mercy for those people whose values are so distorted by the norms of our society that they mistake what is merely peripheral and contingent from what is truly worthy. It is a social tragedy, common in our era. Like most humans, he was so self-absorbed in what was most proximal to him, in only what was immanent, that he was unable to recognize the larger structure of the interconnectedly dependent affairs that were really responsible for his failure in business. He was powerless to affect the strategic maneuverings of such large-scale international corporations; he was not even cognizant of them! He did not have the capacity to clearly recognize what had happened to him. A Buddhist might call it the suffering of ignorance. Instead, he was ready to accept all of the credit, and he internalized all the blame.

It destroyed his spirit, although he continued to be successful at making money from the two television repair stores he owned. He even made a decent profit by making evening house-calls at the homes of some of the biggest Hollywood Stars (Judy Garland, Jimmy Stewart, Dean Martin, etc.), to whom he was their go-to guy when their vanity was threatened by one or more malfunctioning television sets. This more modest success did not prevent him from developing some powerful nervous habits, involving uttering extraordinary noises, clicks, and sounds at inopportune times. And he was never able to fully regain his self-respect. Perhaps that is why the admiration of a younger woman became necessary for him.

Frequently our lives become tragedies. But it cannot be said that these tragedies are not of our own making. Much of the time we fail to understand that the way that the world exists, populated as it is with our conceptual fabrications, is actually *empty* of those fabrications, and that those projections do not exist on their own. That is, the world does not exist the way it appears: we project some comprehensive synthesis of our understanding upon our affairs, and then we think that that is how things really are. My father's failure in business was a product of his imagination, and he did not need to become as depressed by his account of his life as he did. But he was powerless to ascertain the emptiness that undergirds most of the footing that is holding up the stories of our lives. If there is one thing I am sure of, it is that there are no grounds for believing in *any* story about our lives that we tell ourselves. This is why I have always been convinced that suicide is unfounded – it cannot be the case that any formulation of one's life that one devises could have enough validity to merit making suicide a justifiable recourse.

Here the Buddhist dharma suggests that if we cultivate more concern for others than we have for ourselves it can be of great benefit, *for us*. I can recall the comment made to me by the father of one of my childhood friends. I had just graduated college, and I was walking about Beverly Hills with my first serious girl-friend. After walking the length of that small city, admiring each elaborate front yard as if we were walking through a fine museum, we became tired of walking and decided to hitchhike to the beach at Santa Monica. We put our thumbs out, and right away a man stopped to pick us up. He looked familiar to me, as I did to him, and he asked me if I knew his son, who in fact had been a close friend of mine five years previously. When I asked how his son was doing, he told me, "I never worry about my son. He is off in Watts doing volunteer work in a poor black neighborhood. So long as a person is helping others, you will never need to worry about him."

My goodness. It was surprising to hear that kind of wisdom in Beverly Hills. It is the wisdom out of which our truest successes are made. One can conclude that even people who live in Beverly Hills *can* be successful. My father's real failure was to not know much about what really composes success. But I don't blame him for that one either, just as I don't blame anyone who suffers from their own ignorance.

25
The Successful Professor

The professor was quite young for having advanced so far in his profession. Being intelligent and a hard worker – and having excellent discrimination in ascertaining which activities would advance his career and which would impede it – he achieved his full professorship swiftly, and he was now advancing through the lower rungs of the university administration. We were conversing in the faculty parking lot, taking advantage of some moments to enjoy the last rays of sunshine, which with the coming of spring had only in recent weeks at last become available during the post-5pm hour.

My friend was expressing his envy for the freedom of my way of living. Although he was younger than me, his annual income was three times my own (I usually worked only half the year, in order to leave time for practice and for my trips to Asia), yet it turned out that *he* was jealous of my being able to pursue only those studies and research that compelled me deeply. He had chosen to amass position, respect, a large home filled with the latest electronic and computer wizardry, all objectives whose importance and durability he had probably overestimated. As Bob Dylan remarked in one of his early ballads, "Out on Project Hill it's either fortune or fame; you can choose one or the other, but neither of them are to be what they claim." In short, he had not followed his deeper dreams with the same relentlessness that I had.

He shook his head and looked off into Oregon's trees, telling me, "You probably don't know how much people envy you for following your own aims the way you do." I thanked him, wondering to myself how many months he would have been able to survive on rice and lentils daily, how long he would have tolerated bouts of dysentery, how many months he could sleep on wooden beds infested with mites, etc. He smiled and waved good-bye as he stepped into his brand new BMW.

I waved to him in return as I turned towards my twelve year-old Toyota. It is a strange world when the rich people envy those who are poorer, I thought, but for a life that from the start has been based upon envy what other outcome could there be? Envy breeds only more envy, with no predictable end. The good news is that satisfaction breeds more satisfaction. We are free to choose.

26
The Rubber Ball

When my son was hardly a year old and still in diapers, we were living in the Indian hill station of Dharamsāla, where we took full advantage of the love that Indian adults have for children. My son's best friend, however, was an eleven-year old boy from the village who acted as a sort of ad hoc baby sitter, giving us some time to study as they played together in the courtyard. I had purchased a rubber ball and invented a game of handball that captivated the Indian boy. Once I got them going, they could play for several hours. It was as if some magic came to reside in the ball itself. The boy came to revere that ball, and he would turn up for his day care duties ahead of time just to have additional time to play with the handball. In his mind, it had became the origin of all joys.

Buddhists teach that although we project reality upon entities, that projected reality seems to exist as if it was real by itself, inherent in the world. Dogs are also vulnerable to believing their own propaganda. Take for instance the dogs of Sera Monastery, who sleep in the shadows during the day but take over the streets and alleys at night when they administer their policies with growls and confrontations. If they sleep during the nighttime, it is lightly, and any breeze that rustles fallen leaves will awake them. Hearing the slightest disturbance, a dog will bark, at first tentatively. Is there somebody out there? Is there a person or a dog that needs challenging? The barking may awake a second dog, who will bark only because the first dog barked (the second dog herself is awakened too late to hear the leaves rustling). The second dog's barking is accepted by the first dog as confirmation that there really is someone out there, and the first dog will bark again. I explain to my students that just because an utterance is confirmed does not turn that utterance into a truth – for that to happen, one requires the agreement of a third person. Unlike humans, dogs will accept as a truth barking that involves only two (not three) dogs. However, on many nights at Sera there are plenty of additional dogs ready to add their concurring barks to the first two, and once they have done so the crescendo of the pack of barking dogs leaves no doubt about the truth of the independent existence of the intruder, which leads to a howl, moon or no moon, that further objectifies the immanent danger that is demanding a defensive response long after the offending leaves have settled. Eventually the barking too subsides, whereupon the dogs and humans fall back to sleep.

In a similar manner, my son's playmate had made the value of the ball part of the objective nature of the ball itself. The nature of a ball, especially for Buddhists, is surely "empty" of the game of handball – that game would be our own augmentation. But for the village boy the joys of handball resided in the ball itself, part of its resonance as it were. And each day these joys grew only more absolute for the boy. Of course, there was little chance that he could come to realize that he himself was the origin of all that joy (indeed, of all joys), just as there is an equally slim chance that you or I will come to realize that our joys too are our own making.

As the value of the ball kept increasing, the temptation wrought by his fascination became too great for him. One day, my son walked in from the courtyard and showed me that the boy had disappeared with the ball. My son was not upset, only interested to know more about the situation. The boy never returned. I felt sorry for him – in part for missing out on the pleasures of our companionship, which had created the handball festival in the first place, and in part for his loss of payments for his services (which in the end would have included the ball anyway). His own obsessiveness and greed cut him off from what would have been a steady tap of opportunities and congenial relations. It was an example of the delusory practice of superimposing our notions and exaggerating being, an illustration of one of the two extremes of reflection that Tibetan Buddhists have so well identified.

27
The Danger of Attachments

Dusk was falling softly as the Indian child played peacefully with a plastic disc and a push-stick. The disc was a red model of a metal wheel, and the stick was very crude, something found lying alongside the path. It was the sort of combination that I've noticed children playing with all over the world. Years before, I had admired the way that Filipino children were able to push the disc up and back for hours without ever becoming bored. The joy of such play rests in the eye of the beholder, so one need not spend money to obtain such joy, for it rests in the heart of the child.

The Indian boy was about four years of age and had become enthralled with his toy, and the joy it was bringing him was better than magic. While I watched, he gradually learned how to make it roll longer and longer distances, to his increasing delight. Whenever its speed exceeded his control, he would chase after it, always delighted when he caught up with it and brought it under his control once again. On one occasion it went especially far, along the footpath, and he called proudly to his "Mama" so that she would notice it; only this time it went so far down the flat footpath that it ran onto the gravel roadway, and then down that roadway for several yards, until it began to curve toward a steep gully that fell away rapidly to an overhang above a small canyon.

Suddenly spying the steep incline, the child became urgently concerned that his toy might drop into the deep gully and disappear out of sight. He sped after it, obsessed with catching up to the disc as he had done many times before. Just as the disc had exited the road and tumbled down the gully and was about to roll over the overhang, the boy prepared to lunge after it, an attempt that would have resulted in a fall of twenty to thirty feet. Alarmed myself, I shouted out to the boy to stop, just as I had once shouted to my own son when he was two years of age and was about to run gaily into the middle of a busily trafficked city boulevard – my son heard my call and stopped at the curb, thus saving his life. As if by instinct, the Indian boy froze at my command, only inches from disaster.

The boy's father looked up at my shout and then began to scold the mother for not paying proper attention to the boy. He ran to collect him, but the son was unharmed and was only concerned about his disc. The father climbed down the gully to retrieve the disc for him. It was a near miss. The boy's attachment to his insignificant possession had almost led to a major accident; it was only the boy's capacity, a bit tardy, to let go of his attachment that saved him.

Letting go of our attachments can benefit us. How is it that we become so nearsighted in our preoccupation with our petty projects and short-lived affairs? Like that boy, whatever it is that I am intent upon during any given week always becomes an obsession. Although it will surely vanish into emptiness soon and be lost to my awareness, at the time that I am projecting its prominence my engagement with it is all-embracing. What a total lack of perspective I keep generating in my everybody affairs. In his *Yuktisastikavrtti*, Nagarjuna has written,

> In those who believe in entities
> There arises attachment and anger.
> Their views are inexhaustible, they hold on to what is inappropriate,
> And it is from this that disputation comes about.[14]

---

[14] Cited by mKhas grub Je, *A Dose of Emptiness* (*sTong thun chen mo*), translated by José Ignacio Cabezón, New York: SUNY Press, 1992, p. 263.

It is not simply that we fixate upon the ideas we develop about things, and then become attached to those things, whose apparent nature has originated in our own hearts. It is that these views are *inexhaustible*! When *will* they come to an end? *How* will they come to an end? I am old enough to recall how the US almost went to nuclear war with Russia over the missiles in Cuba, a propect that we consider now with incredulity; it could have ended life as we know it. In the same way, each of us is ready to plunge headlong into the pursuit or defense of whatever concretized notion has become the latest mental habit in our mind-stream. The Indian boy is no different from us. We are of one kind – only sometimes there is no one nearby to issue a command that will bring us to our senses.

28
The Two Worst Gifts I Ever Received

When I was a boy I devoted a lot of time to anticipating the presents I would receive for the holidays and for my birthday. There are many aspects to giving presents, including the good that comes from giving; nevertheless, the way that we do it seems to enhance materialism and greed more than it fosters intimate human relations. Especially, heaping piles of presents on special days becomes like a gross exercise that does not contribute much to one's character.

I have an Indian friend who has two yoga schools in Orange County, California, and he has a policy of never giving his two children presents on their birthdays or holidays. He tells me, "If they really want or need something, all they need to do is to ask us for it, and probably we will get for them. We don't require a special giving ceremony for it."

My mother's best friend when I was a teenager was a woman who never stopped talking. Even worse, she had the habit of finishing the final words of your sentence for you, as a device to capture the floor so she could speak some more. But I always received a birthday gift from her, and sometimes they were nice ones since her husband owned a jewelry store. I suppose giving gifts in order to be liked is another aspect of gift giving. Although I did not think highly of her, the gifts balanced her loquaciousness, to the point of my feeling neutral about her.

When I turned 14 years, I received from her a small wrapped box, and I eagerly opened the box to discover the most useless item inside – a small, circular monogrammed leather paper-clip holder 3½ inches in diameter. What possible use could a 14 year old have for a paper-clip holder? I considered it the most useless gift I had ever received. My opinion of her was most promptly demoted to below neutral.

I dutifully kept the paper-clip holder on my desk, probably because it was monogrammed with my initials, though it received little use. I even took it to college, where it began to be used from time to time. During graduate school it became useful, and for the thirty-odd years I was a university professor, it did a good deal of heavy lifting, if paper-clips can be considered heavy. Given the quantity of writing and paper grading I did there were indeed sufficient paper-clips to be considered heavy. From its central position on my desk, that old leather paper-clip holder played a regular and enduring part in my professional life.

It is more than fifty-three years since I was gifted that leather paper-clip holder. Now, even in my retirement it rests on my desk. I have no other gift or possession from my teenage years, only that small leather paper-clip holder. Who could have foreseen this? And that is the point! Most of what we think we know is delusion. We fixate on the meanings of this or that, which we invent; and then we mistake our inventions for the reality. In Tsong Khapa's *Graduated Path* (*lam rim*), he asserts, "One should not critically analyze the actions of another person." When I first read that, I thought it might be extreme, since ethics do sometimes involve critical assessment; however, one must be mindful that the bulk of what we come up with is nonsense, pure invention for which we should not hold the other person responsible. Such mindfulness is a difficult practice, but my poor judgment about the value of gifts suggests it is a reasonable way to avoid being mistaken.

My beloved paternal uncle and aunt always gave me birthday gifts too, up until the time I got married. I was in graduate school when I received a not very attractive cotton/wool/acrylic sweater with a very abstract black-and-white design. I considered it ugly at first sight, and I kept it hiden in my drawer for years without ever wearing it. I began to wear it just around the house, on days that were not cold enough for a woolen sweater. It has the advantage over pure wool sweaters that moths ignore it, so several decades later it was still presentable, while many of my all-woolen sweaters had given themselves up to the moths. In the days after 2000, when black and white became the style, this sweater from the 1970s finally found use as a garment for public use, at dinner parties and barbecues.

I still have the sweater in my drawer today, some 45 years later. I never dreamed that such an ugly sweater would become my most durable piece of clothing, outlasting everything, including belts. This is another case in point. We don't know as much as we think we know, and so we should not become attached to our conclusions. It is best to keep only a loose grip on what we think is true. After all, what world is it in which the two least favored presents of my childhood can become the most beloved and useful ones I ever received?

29
"They Make Hatred At Me"

The train from Salerno to Naples, a fifty-minute journey, was ten minutes late. When I entered the railcar, most of the seats were filled. The only empty seats were three seats that adjoined a fourth seat that was occupied by an Indian-looking lad in the same cell. The fellow was about 25 years of age, and I gladly took the seat as it afforded me an opportunity to learn what an Indian thought about Italy. The others on the train (mostly Italian, though there was a wide multicultural mix of Africans, Turks, Peruvians, and Dutch) had avoided the seat. I presumed that it was partly because the young fellow was quite dark in color, almost black. He was very slight, not more than 125 pounds, and despite being pleasant looking, his color rendered his looks invisible to Italians. He was happy that someone at last was willing to sit next to him, and he offered me some mint-flavored chewing gum, which I accepted. When I took only one piece, he insisted that I take two.

I asked him if he was from India, and he nodded and explained to me that he was from Bengal, close to the border with Bangladesh. He was also Muslim and had come to Italy six years earlier. I considered that it was only an enterprising 19-year old Indian who could have found his way to Europe, and I asked him how he liked Italy. His bearing changed instantly. He said he disliked it. He said the people were cruel and treated him badly: "They always look at me wondering, why does this person come here. They make hatred at me."

After six years of this hatred, the young man had himself become hateful. That demonstrates the influence that others can have upon us. We spoke of his dreams, which included going to Norway as soon as he could get papers, but every time the topic of Naples or Italians slipped into the conversation his aspect changed. He had not even one Italian friend, and he had little chance of finding one. Rarely had I met a person this young with such abject pessimism about life. I wondered whether this could be how many of the immigrants living in Europe felt.

The Italian newspaper I began reading reported about two young Londoners, brothers, who had been convicted of killing a ten-year old Nigerian boy as he returned from a library. This mirrored similar violence in Washington and Philadelphia, and I recalled a recent video that caught on a surveillance camera two white men who beat senseless an elderly Hispanic man. What will be the long-run karmic consequences of so much violence and racial hatred? The two Londoners had been released, but after a long campaign against them they were rearrested; however, eventually a jury of their peers found them not-guilty of murder and convicted them only of manslaughter. How bizarre.

One can have some sympathy, perhaps, for the anxieties of people who may be forced to adapt to the cultures of people who arrive at their doorstep uninvited and mostly unwanted; however, the sympathy ends as soon as their prejudice turns violent. How does one learn to open one's heart to the dissonance of cultures, even when it means changes in one's own culture – tolerating veils at school for instance, absorbing patriarchal traditions of gender, and the like. This is an extremely difficult dilemma because even the host countries are entitled to their own culture.

After a day in the Uffizi Gallery in Florence (a relic of the 16th century), a day that seemed to me more like a season, I walked back out into the street to immediately encounter some Turkish popular music in the Middle-eastern style, which was blaring full blast at the front door of the Uffizi. I happen to love that music and tuned into it instantly. But what is a native of Florence likely to think of it, resounding as a sound track in the face of the Uffizi? And how could a native effectively contest the dissonance in the air of her ancient streets without developing at least some antipathy? The present citizens' war against hard-working poor Mexicans in America, the battle over school dress regulations in France, the cartoons drawn and distributed in the public spaces of Denmark, etc. – where is it that honest contestation, which can accompany accord, be found?

As I stepped off the train in Naples and walked along its streets towards the main square, an African in his fifties was playing guitar for alms in a district of exclusive shops. Sitting next to him were two young Italians around nineteen years of age, who were fascinated with his music and with his life experience. For the present, this African musicians' work was teaching two Italian boys how to love and respect black people, and how to live life more fully. He accepted this responsibility, which was the effect of the sincere and inquiring looks in their eyes, with seriousness and with kindness. The two boys were there only for the afternoon, that much was clear, but so was he. And for the present, it was work *pro bono*, a beggar's own offering of charity to a possible future without racial hatred; and he demanded no compensation. Perhaps human beings will discover their own solutions without their governments. I have always figured that humans will survive only if they deserve to survive.

30
What is the Right Way to Bow?

While people are willing to overlook their own foibles, it is more difficult to accept other people's shortcomings. A spiritual person will accept other people's personal foibles. I am especially unforgiving with people who are dishonest with themselves, who pretend to be something that they're not and who believe their own pretensions. When confronted with a stretch of social disingenuousness, I run for the hills when I should be more tolerant.

There is a flaw with my perspective: *everything* in life has its presentational aspect and so everyday life *requires* a degree of social disingenuousness. When it does, what is disingenuous can go by the name of courtesy, of which I and my fellow Californians are rarely accused. This leads me to the question, why would I spend nearly a lifetime losing faith in other people simply because they are human enough to respond to the social demands that other people in society place upon them? What nonsense is it that I have been up to? Society requires some disingenuousness.

Take bowing, for instance. When one bows, to another person or to a sacred place like a gravestone or an altar, or to a teacher that one respects – the bow can be, and should be, genuine. A degree of humility gets embodied in any bowing, and that can be genuine too. But it is also performance, at least in part. Since bowing involves at least one other person, and occurs in a public space, one is required to display one's humility to others. One's respect is made publicly available by and through the physical routine one uses for doing the bowing. The performance aspect will *inevitably* become entwined with any real humility, to the point that it can become impossible to separate the two.

If one watches how Japanese people bow to each other, one can witness a bizarre competition: the one who is able to bow the deepest is able to publicly demonstrate having the most respect for the other. Since showing respect is held as a high standard in Japanese society, each one tries to outdo the other in winning public approval by being more humble. This sometimes leads to keen competition in self-effacement. This is not to say there is never genuine self-effacement, and it is a treasure when it occurs, but such occurrences may be limited to a minority of the performances. I have witnessed Tibetans compete in self-effacement too, the highest person being the one who is able to successfully engineer taking the lowest seat, and the like. Mostly they engage in such contests as a social form or obligation, without investing too much of themselves in the sport.

Similar duplicity can infect praying. I say "duplicity" because there is *both* genuine sentiment and public performance, which are linked chiasmatically. Prayer can be genuine, i.e. from the heart; and kindness can be what motivates prayer, which is important. But prayer, too, is often performed in public, and so there are accompanying social demands that must be met, like staying in rhythm (if it is a congregational prayer), harmonizing with others, etc. One may feel devotional, but also one must be concerned to display any naturally occurring devotion in publicly sanctioned ways, as a matter of respect for that public, which makes it something that is also not unaffected. Anyone who has prayed has recognized how quickly one's prayer, especially prayers that involve repetition, can become phony, an imitation of themselves. Is courtesy phony? Sure it is, like most things, but that does not make courtesy without utility. Good will makes for good motivation, which is what counts. And motivation is what makes a prayer. But once genuine devotion becomes a simulation of devotion, one can lose track of the original motivating sentiment.

Prostration can be worse, since the humility that motivates it is generally a stronger sentiment than the humility that motivates prayer (that is why people do prostrations). But if any religious act is a performance, it would have to be prostrations, and I have witnessed some brilliant prostraters who can hang their humility out in public space for an endless period of time; some of them are genuine, while others seem to be only performing. Of course, it is difficult to tell the difference; even the performers need to "check up" on their motives and keep limiting the ego-trip aspect of their performance. Such vigilance is always necessary.

Here is where part of my difficulty lies – I cannot myself discern what part of my own bowing to my teacher is my heart speaking and what part is a socially mandated performance, i.e. an act I have learned how to do even when my mind is daydreaming a continent away. On some occasions I simply need to be more mindful and keep reminding myself to keep it real. That too is what we call "practice." On other occasions I abide naturally within its genuine spontaneity. But between these two are the majority of instances in which an honest gesture is *naturally* contaminated with public demands. And for those occasions, it is unreasonable for me to blindly criticize my compliance with social strictures, a compliance that is a regular part of adulthood.

Accordingly, what is even more necessary is for me to accept *other people's* compliance with the mundane demands of the ordinary society they face. And what I need to do is to better learn how to celebrate other people's efforts, despite their being weak enough to bend to everyone's social demands. A spiritual person will love them instead of criticize them.

Of course, cultivating the resolution to do something is easier than actually doing it. As I entertain these reflections, I have been observing a dharma student whose decent reputation is exceeded by her opinion of herself. She is extremely devoted to practice, but to my untutored eye appears to compete in a number of aspects of practice. But this too is natural, and we need to cultivate benevolence toward the people who are sitting next to us in the temple. Unfortunately, as soon as the public recitations are completed, she falls asleep for the actual dharma teaching itself, just as many (sometimes most) Tibetan monks in the monasteries do; and no doubt for the same reason – they have all been up since 4 am praying, and they need to sleep sometime. Regrettably, the sleep comes while a lama may be explaining the important details about analyzing of the emptiness of inherent existence.

Her sleep is quite deep: she is completely checked-out for most of the teaching, a time that most of those around her are making strong efforts to follow each point closely. Her sleep is so deep that in one instance when the lama, who had spent a good ten minutes explaining a subtle point, turned in her direction to ask the people there if they really understood, and he caught her deeply asleep with her head inclined backward and her mouth wide open, pointing toward the ceiling. The lama giggled as a fly circled nearby her, but with not a shred of disappointment in him. The lama's accepting, not disappointed laugh could be a decent instruction to every teacher who has been faced with students who find nothing more valuable in a lecture than an opportunity for a good nap, whereupon it is not unnatural for a teacher to feel some disappointment.

On other occasions this student will only be half-asleep, and she will roll her head around in slow circles while tilting gently forward or to the side; sometimes, a most contorted expression will come across her face, with her forehead crinkling up as if she was receiving the epiphany of Saint Theresa and was entirely overcome with the wisdom she was receiving. The epiphany occurs despite the fact she is not paying more than the slightest attention to the intricate explanations of the lama.

As Ezra Pound wrote in Canto XIII:

And Kung raised his cane against Yuan Jang,
Yuan Jang being his elder,
for Yuan Jang sat by the roadside pretending to
be receiving wisdom.
And Kung said
"You old fool, come out of it,
Get up and do something useful."

"Pretending to be receiving wisdom" would cover the situation. Half-awake and half-asleep, one afternoon the epiphany seemed only to grow stronger. Until finally, when the dharma lesson ended, the student awakened to join enthusiastically in the devotional concluding prayers, including the one about the gratitude for the opportunity to receive bona fide explanations of emptiness. In fact she bellowed the loudest of all, like a schoolgirl. This too had its performance aspect.

How am I any different? Which part of my refuge mudra is really from the heart and which part is pretension? Who has ever offered a religious symbol like a refuge mandala or a simple "How are you?!" that lacked any aspect that was phony? And is not fooling oneself into thinking it is sincere simply a part of the methodology of the yoga, by which one uses the mudra or body position to *improve* one's state of being? *Living requires constant communing with the phony*, so why do I not learn to give people some slack and stop requiring perfection from each person I meet? That may be another reason why forgiveness is given so much importance in all religions.

And for those who cannot forgive, there exists a heavy heart. One can ask oneself, how much generosity of spirit can we afford to offer others? Is there a limit?

31
Seeking Faraway Places

I was visiting my Italian cousins in southern Italy, in the town of Aversa (near Naples), which was established by we Normans following our victory over the Muslims in Calabria and Sicily in the 11th century. My mother's family, who were Normans on both sides, built their houses there long ago, in the 12th, 15th, and 16th centuries, ancient palazzi erected out of the volcanic tuff of Vesuvius, in which my relatives still live today. My cousin Enzo works as an ambulance driver in Aversa, and earlier this morning he was describing to four of his colleagues at work a photograph on my computer that I had showed him, which featured me meditating on a very large rock on my wilderness property in California that sits between two streams that come together to form the main creek that passes by my cabin. Enzo had invited his ambulance colleagues to the ancient family home during their morning break in order to meet his American cousin.

One of his friends, the doctor among them, admitted to me that he had a sincere interest in Buddhism, and he wanted me to describe how the monks who live in Tibetan monasteries spend their time. I immediately recalled the Zen Buddhist *ko-an* in which a monk explains, "Before I gained enlightenment, I would rise in the morning when the bell rang three times, meditate, and then go to breakfast, after which I would wash my bowl. Since I have gained enlightenment, I rise in the morning when the bell rings three times, then meditate, and afterward go to breakfast. When breakfast is finished, I wash my bowl." But I judged that while that account was appropriate to his situation, it would not be appreciated.

Instead, I discussed the monks' prayers, their diet, their studies, etc. I did mention the bell that rings early in the morning every day, offering them my best imitation of its incredible sleep-penetrating cadence. He asked what kind of clothes they wore; since these men were all dressed in the bright orange uniforms of emergency workers, I replied that they wore clothes similar to theirs. But he really wanted to know more about their philosophy and spiritual orientation, so I began to describe a few of the basic beliefs that underlay a Mahayana practice, and I showed him a Tibetan manuscript that I had with me and summarized a few of the themes that it contained. It felt odd to be translating from Tibetan to Italian.

He asked me how I happened to end up in a Buddhist monastery, and I described to him in Italian how I me
root lama in New Zealand in 1975. Being a vegetari
had gone to the only vegetarian restaurant in Christch
There had been a poster on the wall advertising a talk
evening by a Tibetan lama. I had asked the proprietor
it was that an animal could talk, and I suggested
llamas were not from Tibet but from the Andes.
proprietor replied, "No, a lama is a person from Tib
sort of Buddhist priest. Why don't you come al
Fascinated, and still young enough to be eager to s
under every stone for anything that might be useful, I
with him.

The lama (who became my root-lama, Thubten Y
was experiencing some influenza, and he commenc
his broken English by explaining, "I sorry, not so well t
Not speak too much. But I think you know already: a
game means no understanding." I had never before h
such truth spoken so concisely, or so modestly, a
became a Buddhist that instant, even though I am the
who is not inclined to believe in anything. I further expl
to my Italian cousin's friends who were visiting, that
my lama died in 1984, I decided to go to the mor

university of my teacher in order to continue my studies with his teachers, spending three years there over the last three decades.

While we were conversing, my aunt prepared for us some fabulous Italian espresso – a single ounce that bore more flavor than resided inside any Starbucks Grande – and the doctor pined, "I want you to take me with you to your monastery."

"Maybe that's not necessary," I told him. "It is not the case that spiritual stability lives in only faraway places. In fact, most serious spiritual work is best done at home."

He said he was born in Napoli, and all of the others were born in Aversa itself, including my cousin whose direct line of some thirty-some generations were all born in the same house in Aversa as he, in which we were sitting. Imagine: these folk are dwelling in a depth of family and culture, yet they are eager to flee at once to some distant location, some Shangrila, that can exist only in their imagination. Of course, as Ven. Chodron-la told me after reading this manuscript, I myself gained a great deal of insight by going to study in faraway places. But these ambulance workers were like saints, saving lives and aiding the needy, making me bourgeois by comparison. Moreover, these Italians were living in houses that still bear the spirit of their ancestry, that beckons to them daily from beyond their superficial present, even beyond their televisions and jealousies, and yet my cousins want to sell the palazzo and live on the profits. Not only are they are prepared to sacrifice their residence, they are eager to escape their ancestry.

Martin Heidegger writes eloquently about dwelling:[15] "Not every building is a dwelling .... Today's houses may even be well planned, easy to keep, attractively cheap, open to air, light and sun, but – do the houses in themselves hold any guarantee that *dwelling* occurs in them?" Heidegger

---

[15] Martin Heidegger, "Building, Dwelling, Thinking," *Poetry, Language, Thought*, NY: Harper and Row, 1971, pp. 145-161.

describes the condominiums of our era, American houses where people do not spend more than a couple of years in one or another shallow form of residence that lacks any depth or fundamental relation to the earth, such as that provided by the fact that the walls of this ancient house were constructed by the hands of their ancestors out of the Vesuvian volcanic tuff of their yard (the hole that was left behind became their cool storage). Each step of the palazzo's staircases have been worn in the middle by the soles of the feet of our predecessors. Here they not only live, they dwell, in the way that Heidegger describes. And yet my cousins and his friends were oblivious to what they already possessed and were ready to cast it all aside for the very next dream. Just as Heidegger summarizes when he concludes his essay, the real problem is that humans are congenitally homeless: "The real dwelling plight lies in this, that mortals ever search anew for the nature of dwelling." This searching, like that of my cousin and his friends, is without end.

Only my aunt, then 76 years, did not wish to go anywhere. She is fully content to remain in station. Of the 300 members of my extended Italian family living in Italy and the US, she is surely the most extraordinary one: she has understood that changing the externals of one's situation cannot contribute much to happiness, since happiness is something to be cultivated internally and not something to be found in the way that one discovers a precious stone.

It is like the question that her nephew, another cousin of mine who lives in Rome, had asked me earlier in the week. He had experienced many years of suffering due to a wife that he loved very much who was recurringly unfaithful, a situation that ended in a difficult divorce, causing pain to his two children and most of all to him. This rejection has sadly depressed him for years. He found other relationships, but there has always been some sadness surrounding them. It seems that earlier this week, his ex-wife, who is now growing older, has decided that she wants my cousin return to live with her again. After feeling too much rejection over a decade or more, the request itself was a milestone in my cousin's life. Whether her request was only an interest in finding some way to renew her control over the emotions of my cousin, which had begun to lapse, I have my suspicions. Anyway, he now has a new girl-friend from Peru and their relationship is going well, but in a frank conversation he wanted my opinion regarding whether he should return to his ex-wife or continue to live with his girl-friend.

"It makes no difference what you do," I replied to him. "Either choice will only bring further difficulty. Finding happiness is not a matter of changing the external circumstances; only an internal transformation can bring reliable progress, and then it will not matter which of the two you decide upon. Without some internal changes, I assure you, all of your hopes will be lost."

My advice to these men who were visiting was similar. I suggested that they did not need to travel afar but could use their present situation and transform the internal circumstances instead. It is what Buddhists call "skill in means;" however, they were disappointed and somewhat skeptical. So I explained in more detail, "If you wish to seek a spiritual practice, you are already better located than are 90% of the people in the world. Your work in emergency first-aid permits you to offer vital assistance to others on a daily basis. In some cases, the people you help are in extremely dire situations and may lose their lives without your assistance. Work like this is much more powerful for developing a spiritual foundation than simply living inside the walls of a monastery. What is essential for your spiritual development is that *each* time you help others you cultivate some awareness about what you are doing. There must be genuine kindness and generosity of spirit felt *each* time that you help other people by providing them emergency assistance. This will give you many opportunities to develop good motivation, more than most – it will surely enhance the help you bring to many people and, sooner rather than later, bring contentment into your life."

All of them recognized the truth of what I had said, and with a few smiles they reminded each other that the break from their work had gone past its limit and that they must return to their duties. They are fortunate to be living in a situation that produces good karma. So they left the house to spend the rest of the morning helping other people, while I continue to be engrossed in helping only myself.

IV

Modern Times

32
Is Compassion Universal?

I had spent several months giving seminars to graduate students and postdoctoral scholars at Sun Yat-sen University's Institute of Logic and Cognition, and by the end of my seminars the students and I had grown close. These students had an inexhaustible curiosity, a splendid capacity to focus their minds, and they were determined to take advantage of whatever limited scope the Chinese political system offered them for strengthening the democratic opportunities in their society. Although my topics were epistemology, anthropology, and ethnomethodology, all these were focused on the practices of reasoning of various peoples, including Tibetans, and these inquiries necessarily led me to discuss racism – not only the racism inherent in the development of European anthropology, but also the racism that is inevitable in the attempts of the Han Chinese to understand their many non-Han neighbors.

These students displayed surprisingly little racism regarding Tibetans; however, they bore terrific animosity toward the Japanese. One young scholar who had learned to speak Japanese and had even lived in Japan refused to take up any more Japanese studies, simply because he disliked the Japanese so much. Of course, racist sentiments like these operate in both directions, but this is not the place to recount the Japanese innate sense of superiority toward the Chinese (like most of the world's peoples that I have met – even Australian Aborigines – the Japanese feel a natural sense of superiority toward nearly everyone).

During these discussions I raised the topic of racism in America, and I recounted to them a story about George Herbert Walker Bush while he was running for US president against Walter Mondale. Mondale had been criticizing Bush for failing to stand up for human rights while he served as the US Ambassador to China. Bush defended himself by saying, "You don't understand. The Chinese don't value human life in the same way that we do." It was a distorted suggestion that we should refrain from imposing our own values upon other cultures for whom it may be a common practice to brutalize their fellow citizens.

This comment struck me as iconic for the tacit racism that operates beneath the benevolence of most US leaders. In my view, every president until the more recent George W. Bush was a racist, and only two, Bush and Obama, have not been racist. I felt that my Chinese students should be aware, first, of the universality and intransigence of the problem of racism, and second, the even-handedness with which social scientists must criticize racist thinking.

But my students had other ideas. After a long silence, during which I looked at them quizzically, one of the students in the seminar calmly explained, "Bush was right. We Chinese don't value human life the way that Americans do."

The comment floored me, and I was taken aback even further by the reluctant nodding I saw around the table, without any dissent. Had I misjudged the universality of compassion and the commonality of valuing human life? Could it really be possible that George H. W. Bush was right? I didn't know what to say to them, and I simply sat there, dumbfounded.

Returning to my apartment at the university, I could not leave off thinking about it. I am familiar with the international penchant for idealizing American values. Somehow we Americans have managed to sell the idea of freedom and democracy without effectively realizing it ourselves. I first noticed this when I was teaching high school in a Muslim village in the southern Philippines in

1967. The Filipinos dreamed the dream of democracy, and to a great extent put it into action when they overthrew Imelda Marcos in the 1970s. Much the same can be said for nearly every revolution, including the overthrow of the governments in Tunisia and Egypt in 2011. America seems to have an unlimited capacity for inspiring people, despite having recently invaded dozens of countries and having killed hundreds of thousands of innocent civilians while doing so. The scariest part of it is that since Vietnam we have been able to bomb whole villages by increasingly sophisticated remote control, so we no longer need to look into the eyes of anyone we kill. It is an odd version of human liberty.

I remember that this is what most disturbed my professor Herbert Marcuse. He eagerly interrogated me regarding the violence I witnessed in every culture I lived with, and he excused the mild violence of Australian Aboriginal people because, as he put it, "They must witness face to face every victim of their violence, and that makes it more human." Such moral responsibility is no longer an active feature when the violence is inflicted by drones.

But the historical details of the matter do not seem to undermine the faith of most of the world's peoples that America is harboring the possibility of a better future for humanity, including for them. Most every nation I have visited secretly hopes, and some of them actually pray out loud, that one day the United States of America will come to save them. Sometimes I think that the best thing I can do for them is to undermine that faith, so that they can get on with the real business of saving themselves. Another teacher of mine, Ivan Illich, used to argue convincingly that until the poorer nations of the world took on the responsibility of improving their society themselves, without American guidance or any of the directives of modern strategies of economic and political development, they will only become more backward, not less.

Back at my apartment at Sun Yat-sen University I began to consider the history of wars and atrocities in China – the 20 million who died during the cultural revolution, the millions who died during the war that the Chinese fought with the Vietnamese after the Americans left Vietnam, their treatment of Tibetans over the last three centuries, etc. And I had to allow that there was an incredible callousness to it. Further, this callousness is evident in most of the wars that take place around the globe, including the recent uprisings in the Islamic world. I had to conclude that it could be that disregard for human life may be as universal as compassion. And yet I recollected my early discovery while living in that Muslim village, when I was only 19, that everywhere people tend to be kind and to feel a responsibility to extend their hospitality to others, a realization that led me to conclude at that young age that I had little to fear from my fellow humans: human beings were basically good. I remember reporting that news to my mother upon my return from the Philippines. Most people in every village I have visited – in Indonesia, Central America, southern Italy, southwestern China, central Australia, southern India, etc. – instinctively treat visitors with kindness. I cannot even except New York City.

Considering my Chinese students further, I suddenly realized that their admission that the Chinese do not value human life the way that they should was in fact clear evidence of just the opposite! My thinking went like this: these students were appalled at the history of callous indifference to violence in their own country, an indifference that perhaps had dwelled in the hearts of their people, but they genuinely aspired to something that was more compassionate, more ecumenical, more tolerant, more responsible, and more kind. They themselves were dreaming a dream of universal justice, of human rights and democracy, and somehow that dream has come to be embodied – albeit in a conflicted way – in the United States of America. In their imagination they have dreamed that the American people are more compassionate and have more regard for the preciousness of human life than what they have witnessed in their own society during their lifetimes. But that does not constitute their actually valuing human life *less* than Americans do, in the way that George H. W. Bush asserted. It is certainly not the case that an advocacy for more human rights was nowhere in evidence among Chinese.

What was in the hearts of these young Chinese scholars? Dilemmas like this one may be the reason why I like to travel. Do the Chinese have a diminished view of the value of human life? Positively not! By agreeing with the elder President Bush's criticism, my students only provided proof that his criticism was erroneous. They value human life dearly, and they dream that everyone should value human life dearly as well. Their rejection of my assessment was only evidence that they were determined to try to change the world until a state of affairs was established where compassion can become a universal value. This dream, which is *their* dream, is alive and well.

33
Buddhist Environmentalism

If you can catch a Mexican off guard or after a couple of beers, you can sometimes learn from them what they really think about Americans. Of course, they do not call people from the U.S.A. "Americans," since it is their view that the appellation "American" can be applied to every person who lives in North America and South America. The Mexican newspapers call people from the United States "*Estadounidenses*," which means "people from United States." Of course that ignores the fact that Mexico's full name is "The United States of Mexico," but they do not permit the rhetoric of political correctness to become an infinite regress. More ordinarily, Mexicans call Americans "*gringos*," and the land from which the *gringos* come from is sometimes referred to as "*Gringolandia*." I myself come from Gringolandia.

Gringolandia is a particular sort of place, bearing many things both good and bad. One trait of Gringolandia that most Mexicans have noticed is that most *gringos* have a visceral distaste for insects, almost to the point of paranoia. It is true that Americans generally prefer to kill insects on sight, rather than learn to live with them. A few Mexicans have associated this instinct to exterminate insects with the way that *gringos* invade countries. I have heard the thought expressed that possibly the paranoia that motivates both kinds of activities may derive from the same character. When I heard my Mexican friends speak in this way, I was reminded of a saying I once heard in an American Indian community in Montana about the policy of the first Europeans who settled the American West.

According to their account, during the period of European settlement of America there was a two-fold policy: "If it moves shoot it, and if it doesn't move chop it down."

Many of my American retiree neighbors in Baja California Norte, where I have my home, do indeed follow such a policy. Since rabbits, quail and rattlesnakes move, they are shot. On this rancho it is only on my plot where they are left alone, so my plot is a kind of animal refuge. And since the coastal chaparral plants (including sage, rabbitbrush, dune globemallow, a sort of aloe vera plant called live-forever (*Dudleya*), incensio, jojoba agave, sand verbena, etc.) do not move, they get chopped down. Each year we receive a short period of rains, and the plants grow back all on their own; and every year my neighbors hire Mexican workers to chop the ground back to the bare earth. Or, they wait for the plants to dry out and set a torch to them. The yards of most of my neighbors appear as if a scorched earth policy was strictly enforced. That is, until you cross onto my property, where all of the plants are permitted to do whatever is their natural inclination, without molestation—leaving what my neighbors consider to be "an unsightly mess." But it is a mess that I dearly love. I don't even clear out the dead century plant stalks. I figure if it is there, it belongs there, and I prefer to watch it in order to learn what it does, over time. It turned out that what dead century plants do is provide a roost for hundreds of birds daily, which comes in handy for them when one of my neighbors' cats come prowling. Their cats like my place too, since it has more life.

The average American who comes here will remove their plant cover the first time they get caught in a patch of "jumping cactus" (known as *cholla*) and get a load of spines in their fingers. Life is safer that way. More secure. The plants on my land are allowed to do their own thing, and I generally have more flowers (with zero watering required!) than do my neighbors, who have a preference for ice-plant, lawns, and tropical palm trees. Rabbit and quail, along with the rattlesnakes that chase them, thrive in this vegetation. And I don't mind a few rattlesnakes, since they always mind their own business, leave at the approach of anyone, and belonged here before I did. Also, they play a role in keeping the rodent population under control. Yes, call me an eccentric as my neighbors do, but I prefer to view myself as pro-life. I genuinely love the wild "bush" on my property. And I have noticed that many Mexicans feel very happy to see it when they visit me.

But this year I experienced a difficult challenge to my policy. Each spring, after the miniscule rains are over, there is an annual swarming of bees. Naturally, it occurs just when the coastal chaparral flowers are peaking. And because I have more flowers than anyone else around, the bees seem to prefer to seek out their season's lodging near my house. One year they took up residence in a hollow century plant stump. Last year they took over the storeroom-cum-hotwater heater room next to my house. It was a nice, warm secure place for them; but since it interfered with the work I needed to do in my storeroom, I smoked them out with some Tibetan incense that had gone stale, and then I constructed screens to prevent them from reentering through the ventilation hole for the heater, as they had been doing. It worked nicely, and they did not return.

This year they came back again, only to find an even stronger network of screens (I was ready for them in time) obstructing their free passage. However, I had just completed a new room on my roof, and one afternoon I found about a hundred bees *inside* the new room, even though none of the windows were open. The new room included a bathroom, and after some investigation, I discovered that the bees were entering through a small hole made for fitting the sewage outflow pipe. So I caulked the holes with silicon, stalling their entry.

As part of the construction for the "roof room" as I call it, we had to level off the pitch of the roof and then build a new, flat floor on top of the roof. This left about four to twelve inches of airspace between the top of the old roof and the underside of the new room's floor. Since we did not caulk the underside of the holes for the plastic plumbing, three tiny holes remained through which bees could enter the airspace between the roof and the floor. Although they were blocked from entering the new upstairs room, by the time I learned that the bees had discovered that airspace—after hearing massive buzzing above the ceiling of my downstairs study—there were a thousand bees crawling alongside each other in three large hanging bags of bees, waiting to get into that airspace.

I freaked. And I freaked in a very *Gringolandia* way: I wanted to kill all of the bees as soon as I could figure out a safe way to do it. Safe for me, I mean.

The last time I had seen such large sacks of bees was when half a dozen similar such hives were erected at the entrance to the main prayer hall of Sera Monastic University, a Tibetan Buddhist monastery where I have lived many years. At the time, I was amazed that a thousand monks could go in and out of those doors daily without anyone bothering to remove the hives. When I asked some of the monks who served as custodians why they didn't remove them, they told me that it was very "auspicious" to have beehives in front of an entrance. After all, these were Buddhist monks! Several monks were stung each day, and the bees had been given free run of the meditation hall, which did not always serve to enhance the monks' meditations. I was impressed with the monks' kindness and patience, but I was glad that I didn't have bees where I meditated.

Now I had them.

I told my contractor that we needed to purchase some poison, shoot it into the airspace and then caulk the bottom of the holes for the plastic plumbing. This would prevent them from occupying my home. I must admit frankly that I was excited, even a bit frightened, and wanted to retrieve a sense of security by killing the bees and making it impossible for them to survive alongside me.

From where did such paranoiac ravings spring? My let-the-earth live philosophy was exposed as pitifully thin.

My contractor and friend, said to me, "Why don't you just let them live?" I replied, "What do you mean?" He explained, "When they come to my house, I like to have them. It's good to have them around. They don't interfere with anything you are doing, they are only interested in gathering pollen. And they're *hard* workers. They *always* work hard. I admire them."

I was convinced by his comments. I was also impressed by what I instantly recognized to be his very broad and wise perspective on living. I reflected that it was good that my experience with the Tibetans had prepared me well for the cultural surprise of a policy that would commend living alongside other sentient beings! But as I gave the comments further consideration and saw the bees swarming by the many, many hundreds, I freaked once again. I answered, "No, let's wait until nightfall when it gets cold, and then let's plug up the entrance." My friend/worker explained that we couldn't just leave the bees trapped inside alive since there was no predicting what they would do next: "They'll find some way out and get into another part and find another entrance. Bees are smart!" I considered this and decided to buy some poison, so that they would not be trapped alive, and by then my neighbors began to arrive with their recommendations about the best poisons to use in the circumstances. It was as if they stood in united opposition to an insect species that in fact had more rights to the territory than we did.

I returned to my study to wait until nightfall. But I kept considering the issue. I recalled a lecture one of my Tibetan teachers, Lama Zopa Rinpoche, gave about living with ants. "Don't worry about them," he said. "They go and come and have no interest in your affairs." This advice had served me well in many situations. But to be perfectly frank, I am more an American than I am a Buddhist, at least regarding spiders, mosquitoes and such things. Any scorpion in or near my house will die. I began to question just what sort of bodhisattva practice is it that I practice?

I considered, "What damage can the bees cause me?" They were not returning to my storeroom where I sometimes work, and they had been obstructed from entering the new roof room. They were now confined to a space that was of no use to me. And bees provide a good deal of benefit by pollinating the flowers. Where would humankind be without them? I had just been reading that California bees were endangered due to a new mite, and that if they continued to decline, agriculture could be faced with a disaster. I thought, "If the bees are not going to damage me, what moral right do I have to harm them?" [Note carefully—if they *were* to do damage to me, by returning to my storeroom, for instance, I would always consider my own interests supreme, and kill the bees wantonly. So my practice of compassion here is pitifully pedestrian.] Now there was no longer any harm in my way! So was I over-reacting? Also, I kept wondering *from where does so much fear and violence come.* This kind of self-inquiry is also an important part of Buddhist practice.

I resolved to try to improve my concern for other sentient beings by learning to live with the bees. One way to break down the dualism that divides my thinking from nature is to permit nature to invade my space and demand me to be the one who readjusts, in both physical and conceptual ways. The earth had approached me very close this time, but perhaps it was an opportunity for me to learn. On the one side stood Tibetan culture and Mexican culture; on the other side stood the violent wisdom of *Gringolandia.* Did I not want to transform that violence? What better place to begin than with my own heart?

I went back upstairs and told my Mexican friend and repairman that I decided he was right. I should just try to learn to live with the bees. Not only live with them, he suggested, but I could even celebrate all the good work I am helping them perform by assisting them in their work of making the countryside flourish. My own contributions to my habitat pale next to those of the bees!

I think I'm on the right side this time. Since my decision, most Mexican visitors I have had have admired the hive, and most gringo visitors have questioned my sanity. As the weeks have progressed, the high volume buzzing that was once so intimidating has become a reassuring sound. I have even learned to do *sirshāsana* (the headstand) while they are buzzing around my nose, occasionally landing! I am a more active participant in the earthly events going on around me, which is the kind of "environmentalism" that Buddhist practice naturally services.

34
The Emptiness of the Forest

When I was still a young man, my wife and I spent five years living and traveling in central Australia, Nepal and India. When we finally returned to the US in 1979, we decided to purchase some wilderness property to use as a base for retreat and to help keep us from becoming too fully reconnected to urban American consumerism. With the help of one of my oldest friends, who worked for the US Forest Service in northern California, we found a tract of land that was surrounded by wilderness areas. Located at 3,000 feet of elevation, approximately half-way between Mt. Shasta and the Pacific Ocean, it had been a successful gold mine during the first decade of the 20th century, so it became patented land that was ineligible for wilderness status and excised from the forest. That made it perfect to purchase for a retreat site – the only neighbors were pine martens, deer, bears, cougars, and steelhead, and plenty of them.

The land was located adjacent to the square mile on earth that biologists have determined has the greatest number of different species of conifers (pine, spruce, fir, etc.) of any square mile on earth; and it featured a small cascade-cum-waterfall that spills into a large pool where one can drink the fresh water as one swims. There are in fact half a dozen pools on the property and another dozen or so adjacent, with incredible stands of conifer, oak, dogwood, maple, alder, and an understory of verdant celery (two species), sorrel, miner's lettuce, and a diminutive *Madia* that each spring lends a Juicy Fruit™ smell to the place for a month each year. When I gaze upon these seven acres from the top of the nearby 5,000 ft. knoll directly above (about an hour's climb), "my" stand of forest is clearly the healthiest stand in the entire watershed – the tallest, greenest, best watered, and richest trees of a very rich forest. Right away I fell in love with the place. After nearly four decades it has become the most stable location of my life, exceeding the tenure of even my storage unit. It grounds my life, including the periods when I am not there.

Looking back upon the first months of my ownership, I am compelled to reflect upon how arrogant I was regarding the place. Although even then I declared somewhat theoretically that no one could "own" the earth, I still felt as if I was all-important and the land was entirely subject to my stewardship: the trees stood straight for my sake, the firecracker flowers turned red each July for my eyes, the huckleberries ripened for my tongue, and the water roared or gurgled for my ears. Although I respected everything, all of these natural forms gained their value mostly by reference to my empowering gaze. I was what was consequential, and the natural forms were subject to my domination.

It is interesting to consider how objects take on meaning. Even though each phenomenon derives its significance from the sense that we project upon them, things are taken as if they bear those meanings in-themselves. That is, *we miss the fact* that *we* have produced the sense that the world has. Even though our projections originate from our own imaginations, somehow their links to our minds get severed and they are mistakenly taken to exist *on their own*, in the very ways that we have imagined them. Buddhist thinkers say that these things lack any inherent existence that is based upon the meanings that we project upon them. This is the meaning of "emptiness" in Buddhism – things are empty of what we have projected upon them. For Mahayana Buddhists, emptiness is not some universal god or something absolute that floats about somewhere up in the sky; rather, emptiness is always an emptiness of something in particular. For instance, if I think this tree is "beautiful," its beauty is not something it possess in-itself from its own side, as some intrinsic essence. That tree itself is "empty" of that beauty, which I have lent to it. One recalls the saying, "Beauty is in the eye of the beholder."

Similarly, consider the constellations of the nighttime sky. Humanity has organized the stellar arrays into pictures or gestalts that are made the basis of their identification – Cassiopeia, the Big Dipper, Pegasus, Scorpius, etc. Once one is schooled, any gaze immediately groups the stellar array according to the appropriate constellations assigned to them. Do these constellations exist in themselves? When I was first taught them, I thought that they were. Later I learned that some of the stars that inhabit these constellations reside further away from their fellow stars than they do from earth, which renders the coherence of a constellation strictly perspectival. The truth is that the stars have no relations with each other, astrology notwithstanding. Their constellation – Hercules, Argo – is only a conceptual projection that we impose and that has no inherent essence of its own. In other words, those constellations' natures are empty, in that they are empty of whatever inherent essence we have projected upon them. They do exist, but not in the way that they appear to our fabricating minds. Some evenings I undertake the following exercise as a sort of emptiness meditation... I try to gaze blankly at the nighttime sky and stare long enough for the stars to *lose* the imposed organization I have learned and flood back into disorder. After some moments, suddenly a swarm of stars will appear in the sky, as the stars recede into their anonymity, which, like ourselves, is their actual nature. Those are the stars just as they are (this is their "thatness" or "suchness," Tib. *de kho na nyid*); such a display overwhelms one's senses and freshens one's outlook.

Let's consider further the example of the forest. There are many ways to understand a forest. To a religious person, it is God's work, and I have heard ministers explain to their congregation camping in a grove of a national forest that God may be witnessed in the way the sunlight splashes through the trees in beams or shafts of light. An animist or druid, like those of prehistoric Europe, might believe that spirits inhabit the trees, and this regard causes animists to develop considerable respect for the forest. Even in contemporary India, both Hindus and Buddhists have sacred trees that are believed to bear spirits, even though such spiritual content is only a projection of how they understand trees. Contemporary environmental activists like the members of Earth First! also project a kind of spiritual content onto the forest – and then come to believe that those spiritual properties are born by the forest in-itself, entirely separate from human conceptualizing.

Foresters make similar mistakes. I know many people who have lived in Siskiyou County, California, for several generations who apprehend the forest in terms of cubic board feet. They think the forest truly exists *in itself* just that way they have conjured it. When they visit my cabin and point to some of the larger trees, and tell me, "Oh my goodness, that's a $5,000 tree you have there!" the trees of my forest are thereby transformed into a bank account. Even after my friends depart I keep going on in that way, thinking silently to myself for instance, "Oh, that one must be at least a $3,000 tree!" All of a sudden the *meaning* of my forest has been transformed. I suppose if a military general were to visit, my land would become a site for strategic opportunities; and there is no end to the possible "realities" that the land can bear. But the point of emptiness is that *none* of these imputed realities exists as an *intrinsic* part of the forest's being.

Just what is the trees' real being, then? Contemplating this question has been my task for four decades, and I seem to be much better at refuting answers than locating them. Two years after we first bought the property my wife's sister and brother-in-law, whose professional occupation was tree-trimming, made a visit to the land and reported to us, "This place is a mess! No one has taken care of it; things are overgrown everywhere." The notion that there had to be someone to look after a wild place brought a smile to my face. The brother-in-law offered us this proposal: he would trim all of the trees of our natural forest and "clean the place up" in exchange for a percentage of the property; given the extensive amount of work that was involved, he suggested that 50% would be about the right amount for the split.

I replied quickly, before he had any chance to act: "You are welcome to visit the place, but please do not touch even one branch!"

The incident helped me to resolve not to touch a tree myself for the first decade of my stewardship, while I allowed the place to me teach me what it was. Accordingly, I did not alter a thing for a full decade. After ten years I began pulling up Douglas fir seedlings and young maple shoots, since they were suffocating the oaks that the Native American residents I had befriended valued so highly. Although the Native Americans' view too is their biased perspective, thanks to some remaining descendants of the original inhabitants I had begun to learn to view the land from their perspective, and so began to feel protective of the several oak species that the Indians considered precious. Also, I had learned that the fir and maples obstruct the flow of the riverside breezes that are essential for keeping the mosquitoes down to an unobjectionable level.

What Endures

The tree fell early one spring,
looking fresh with all its pine needles.
Its length blocked our trail to the pool
beneath the falls,
but instead of moving it to the side
we moved the trail
and skirted around it for 30 years
while we studied its decay.

About 15 years after its fall,
it reached its peak –
its insides lay open
for a lush window box garden of flowers and ferns.
A series of delicate flowers found their way
to its decaying heart-wood.

Then came years of flood,
then years of fire,
and it never regained its commanding presence.
When I returned after a year in Asia,
it was mostly not-there,
and the old trail to the pool
could be used again.
What was evident was the void
that had been lying underneath it,
of which it might be said,
nothing endures.

After I had begun to learn the land's ways, I felt entitled to make a few alterations. After 20 years, I began to clear some of the hazel nut and the lower branches of the conifers and oaks that grew close to the cabin, to afford the cabin some open space in the event of a fire. For that reason I also began a regime of annually raking and burning the leaves in the vicinity of the cabin, so they would not carry a fire to the cabin's foot.

Humans are able to dominate a landscape: that is a simple task. But to learn from the landscape what it is *on its own* – what are its own ways and natural tendencies – takes time and considerable attentiveness since our thinking, whatever that is, keeps getting in its own way.

For 15 years I owned some property on the Oregon coast. Since the Oregon seafront weather is so hard, with the sun rarely shining, most people who came to live there did not remain for more than a few years. By the time ten years had passed, I had become the oldest resident on the street. It was a beautiful place, set in natural shorepines, salal and pinemat Manzanita, and white sand dunes. My favorite spot was a hundred yards upshore where a shorepine had been twisted in bonsai fashion by the steady winds, making a kind of natural cave in the vegetation of the sand dune inside of which one could gaze at the ocean without being blown to bits by the wind. It was so charming that someone bought that site and placed a house right on the spot, bulldozing the very charm that had attracted them. They moved away two years later, unable to tolerate the steady gale force winds.

But I am not so different in the way that I discount the independence of the trees near my wilderness cabin. I think, "Everything here is subservient to me. I choose which trees are to be cut and which are to be left standing. The gold that sits at the bottom of my pool, or the flakes of gold that are enwrapped about the cocoons of the caddis flies like some golden armor, are there only for my benefit, to exploit or not, as I see fit! The celery is there for me to eat, the fish for me to catch, or not; I am everything, while its being is contingent upon me! Despite my wilderness ethic, I have still made myself the center of all activity, and is that not true for much environmentalism? Our arrogance is really inextinguishable. How beneficent is our custody! Without us, how would they ever become noble trees?" Despite my appreciation of the emptiness of how a "forest" is understood, the importance of my "I" has been left undiminished, possibly enhanced, even as I brag about understanding emptiness!

When I bring friends to visit the cabin, I lead them on a wilderness tour like I was a guide in a museum or the conductor of an orchestra for whom the boulders, trees, and cascades are my instruments, features whose destiny is to exist for me! Despite my efforts, I am unable to escape this fundamental distortion, or to truly witness the emptiness of the forest, which is every bit as empty as the nighttime's stellar array.

What *is* the emptiness of the forest?

Although I have some intellectually acquired appreciation of how the forest is empty of the ideas I have projected upon it, including the aesthetic properties I project onto it, I have *not* accomplished – despite this late stage of my life – what the Mahayana Buddhists have named a "direct view" of the emptiness of the forest, whereby at the more innate and subtle levels I no longer distort the reality of the situation, but witness the forest only "the way it is" and nothing more.

Having reached a time when I recognize that I do not possess the infinity I imagined that I possessed the year I had acquired the property, I have at least gained some insight into the fact that my hegemony over my wilderness property is limited, not nearly as considerable as I had imagined. I have come to realize that the noise of the river as it falls down through the boulders at my waterfall, which formerly had existed only to insure me a restful sleep, will in a short time (when I have no existence at all) be the noise of the river laughing at my haughtiness to have ever entertained the notion that I was its possessor. Although I have comprehended little, I still have a bit more time to purify my mind of more of the projected ideas that I have built about the place, time for trying to cultivate a direct experience of the emptiness of the forest.

I am not even certain how to commence, since *any* formulation is simultaneously contamination. That is one of the abiding ironies of living. It is like the tree that falls when no one is there. What is the forest's bare existence? Even the name "forest" disappears.

35
Birds of a Feather

Some months I spend more time relating with birds than I do with humans. The prolific *frutilla* bushes (a fruit-bearing type of buckthorn) that grow on either side of the sandy approach to my front door harbor two species of rabbits and a variety of birds, including junkos, quail, and several seed-eating species I am unable to identify. I am always impressed with how harmoniously they share the same living quarters. When the *tecolote* (eagleowl) circles overhead in search of a meal, the rabbits and birds all rush inside the *frutilla* bush for protection.

Not only do they share the quarters, they communicate with each other about intruders, a process of communication in which the ground squirrels (who have their own homes underground) join the fraternity. When my neighbor's cat approaches, a ground squirrel notices, signals to the junko, who alerts the quail, who broadcast the warning to the rabbits. Usually all of them have found safe cover inside the buckthorn before the cat, stalled in the face of all this opposition, is able to intrude closely upon the scene.

My landlord, who imagines turning this remote Mexican rancho into a suburbia-like park of lawns and tidy rows, wants me to tear out all of the *frutilla*; but for twenty years I have regularly refused his request. I don't have the heart to place my animal friends in danger. He also presses me to tear down the dead agave stalks (century plant) in order to make the place look "cleaner," but those dead floral stalks at its top have great utility for the flycatchers and mockingbirds, whose song I especially love, although I would prefer that they change their repertoire more frequently.

Persistence

How many centuries
    have these mocking birds
sat atop these agave spears
    singing these satiric verses?
Long before
    I ever reached this place.
Long after
    I am gone,
    and this house has disintegrated to rubble.

Or will they find a different song at last?

Most of all, when a hummingbird alights next to a tanager (during the latter's annual visitation) in the uppermost dead agave branch, the "dead" stalk more than proves its worth as a living part of the process.

Two years ago I erected a bird-bath for the birds, who delight in it, especially during the dry times, which is most of the year here in Baja California Norte. In the last year, a couple of the junkos have come to adopt me, and they no longer run away when I fling open the front door; on the contrary, my appearance brings them closer since I frequently toss out to them the crumbs from my table and counter. Even when I have no food, they follow me around my lot, expecting things from me and carefully studying my ways. My large lot is one of the few here to remain wild since I allow little to grow that is unable to find its way here on its own. I like to leave open my front door in the mornings, to let the sun stream in, and on occasion a bird or two will enter my house to forage; they seem to have lost their fear of me.

A team of biologists discovered recently that rats in the laboratory commonly display feelings of compassion. Yes, "feelings," their report said. In repeated tests, rats bypassed food in order to rescue other rats who were in trouble. Occasionally, the rats would quickly snag a piece of chocolate along the way, but they would wait to eat it until their fellow rat was freed, and then they would share the chocolate with the friend. How is it that we automatically reduce such beings to third-person phenomena (he/she/it) when they too are looking out for others' welfare?

What is meant here by the word "automatically"? Our language itself has already reduced these sentient beings to *things*: even as I typed this paragraph my word program underlined the word "who" in the second sentence of this paragraph, instructing me to change it to "that." This was automatic. The grammar of our language will not allow rats to be rendered as intentional beings. What egoism Judeo-Islamic-Christian humanity bears! The very religions that purport to teach humility inflate the importance of human beings beyond what we are entitled to, ontologically speaking. And this same egoism is leading us to destroy the habitats that protect our fellow species. Half of the world's species, both plant and animal, have become extinct during my lifetime.

My neighbor has for years enforced a scorched earth policy that permits no plant to grow in his half-acre lot. As soon as some plants regenerate themselves during the very early spring that comes here (which commences in mid-January), this American destroys them. His sense of what genuinely belongs extends not much further than to the couch next to his television set or the plastic chairs on his front porch. Truly, the real foreigner here is himself. After all, this is Mexico. The quail and rabbits, both of which he shoots regularly, have found safe refuge on my half-acre.

For all this, I am appreciative of the interest that the junkos have taken in me. Even though their primary motive may be greed, they seem willing also to keep learning more about me. Two of them in particular, with unique markings, have adopted me. I have in my study a painting of a venerable Buddhist sage from Tibet who is depicted with a deer and cranes alongside him, to whom he is feeding the fruit from his tree. Cranes are the most timid of all birds. I have learned this in Baja California. Each day, when I enter the water with my surfboard, the cranes depart the very first moment that I appear with my board, whereas the pelicans, ducks and grebes have grown accustomed to my presence. The blue cranes we have here along the shore are able to detect me even *before* I actually appear, they have a second sense that way, and they take flight instantly. They will brook zero companionship with any human. Occasionally, I can sneak up on them by riding the whitewater in to shore while remaining in a prone position on my surfboard, especially if the wind is offshore. However, there are loons who will tolerate my surfing alongside them when the fish beneath us are feeding them well, and the pelicans, a self-confident species that bears little fear, have accepted me in their stride for more than a decade now.

Sea gulls are tolerant but incredibly stupid. When I feed them spare food scraps, I try to bring enough so that even the weaker ones can get a morsel. If there are 20 sea gulls and I bring 30 morsels and toss them all out at once, taking care to spread them around widely, instead of each gull getting a scrap the bully gulls will threaten to attack any weaker gulls who attempt to feed (oh here is that computer program again warning me against using "who" for a bird – you see how ingrained inside the grammar is our species bias?). But in order to impose his doctrine of fear, the bully gull cannot afford to distract himself long enough to eat! So it becomes a lengthy standoff, during which no one benefits. This standoff can persist for half an hour, a true comedy, with the food sitting there without a single gull enjoying it. Usually, I become fed up with them before much eating occurs, and I return home.

The gulls' main food supply lives in the rocks of the point, near where I surf. One morning this week they were feeding as I slid into the water with my surfboard. Both the feeding and the waves were excellent. They squawked at my presence, in the same way they do to each other when I feed them, perhaps worried I myself may try to compete with them for a morsel. They all flew up, circled above my head, and as if on a signal, simultaneously shat upon me. It was as if hailstones were falling, and I was grateful that I was wearing my hooded wetsuit! I remembered an elderly Aboriginal man once describing to me this avian tactic, including a Dreamtime tale about it, but this was the first time that I had experienced it for myself.

Many of the other bird species have tolerated me better, and there is little doubt that most of our birds here recognize me. Birds are even capable of distinguishing kind folks from nasty ones, and they may even communicate to each other about it or at least indicate the level of relative threat (friend or foe) of an approaching human. I have convinced myself that I am receiving good ratings.

In India small birds willingly approach humans, or at least do not fly away at their arrival the way most birds in North America do. Indian boys do not throw stones at birds, whereas many kids in North America are unable to imagine a different way of relating with avian life. Take for instance the fear of humans displayed by most birds in the US, relative to Asia. It is a clear condemnation of our way of life, exposing Americans as more violent than many people elsewhere in the world. Of course, I have little power to change this. But I am at least trying to cultivate a few friendships with the birds who live on my lot.

Now that we've had some rains, the *frutilla* bushes are finally flowering, and many hummingbirds are visiting them each day, methodically visiting each one of the tiny inflorescences, which will turn into deliciously sweet small round red berries that none of the gringos here wish to eat. I wonder how long it takes for the plant to refresh the nectar after a hummingbird has siphoned it. The bees also feed abundantly from the flowers of these plants that my landlord wants me to remove. The *frutilla* provides a good deal more life to the place than do I, or than my landlord does. Another neighbor of mine was attempting to defend me to my landlord, in Spanish, and tried to explain to him why I am so eccentric about not wanting to remove "undesirable" native plants; however, after some conversation, he failed to make much progress. Then he concluded, "Well, maybe you cannot understand it. But you do have to respect it because it is his religion." I hadn't thought of it exactly that way, but the more I reflect upon it, the more I agree with his point.

36
Surfing Ethics in Guanacaste

I had been surfing Witch's Rock on the weekend, camping at Playa Naranjo adjacent to Costa Rica's premier surf break instead of boating in, in order to better absorb the feel of that magical place where the howler monkeys dwell. The week had been devoted to Spanish language study in Tamarindo, predominantly drills with the subjunctive tense and irregular verbs in the past conditional tense, and so I gave myself over to wilderness surfing for the weekend. My plan after two months of coursework was to spend a third month exploring the other famous wave in Costa Rica – Pavones, in the south of the country, which is one of a handful of places on earth that lays claim to having the longest ride in the world, a left that is one kilometer long.

Then I read the following description of Pavones in the "Surf-the-Planet" travel guide to Costa Rica, written by Felix Bracco and Matían Guzmán, two Argentinan surfers (Buenos Aires: Surf the Planet, 2004):

> Pavones is generally always crowded, and not only by locals. You won't believe how great this wave is, and you won't believe the bad vibes that you get when in the water! On a good day for surfing you might find 150 at the spot, spread out along the break. Nobody is laughing, everybody looks serious, very focused. The reason? Everybody is vigilantly hoping that the one riding the wave will fall down or that the lip will break his or her board into pieces, so that someone else can be the new owner of the amazing wave.

> And it doesn't end here ... even more depressing is to see foreigners who, because they've been living here for some time, think they are the owners of the break. They argue, they are rude, and they control the "surf transit" as if they were the Kings of Pavones. They don't even know how to speak Spanish and they decide who surfs and who doesn't .... Idiots. The result: the inevitable; everybody hates each other and wishes the worst to the next one ... the energy at the peak is really negative: with 70 or so surfers thinking, "Please make him fall!" It provokes the worst results! In addition, when you are surfing, you can't share it with anybody else ... the surfing essence is lost, wasted.

This was the most damning description of a surf break I'd ever read. I showed it to half a dozen friends who had surfed Pavones, and they all told me, "That's exactly how the place is!" So I cancelled my plans to visit there.

Since Costa Rica was experiencing heavy rains, except for Guanacaste, even during this "dry season," I decided to spend my spare month in southern Guanacaste instead, and I rented a car with some friends in order to explore some of the more remote and lesser known breaks there.

We had a blast! Camping with the turtles, we surfed mostly by ourselves. We surfed the breaks from the north of Guanacaste to the south, making only a few dozen kilometers of progress each day. We finally reached Malpais at the southern end of Guanacaste, entering it from the less developed northern end after some serious river crossings in our 4x4. Since most people enter Malpais/Santa Teresa via the paved road from the south, its northernmost 2-3 miles is less populated, so the first of Malpais' breaks we pulled into – Playa Hermosa ("Beautiful Beach," one of many Costa Rican beaches with this name) – was empty. It also afforded excellent camping in a forest canopy-cooled beachfront zone.

What is it about surfing that can create bad vibes in the water? Surfing in a spiritual way can make it a friendly sport, a spirituality that "can be shared" with others, as the Surf-the-Planet authors suggest. Since it is not a cooperative activity like a team sport but performed by individuals, there is much scope for competitive individualism, and it even seems even natural to it. If the truth be admitted, surfers are not the most generous people in the world, at least when they are in the water. Cultivating a generosity of spirit while in the lineup is a formidable spiritual practice, but this is only a theory since I've never been able to practice it; moreover, demonstrating generosity is also a quick way to be considered a loser by those other surfers who stand to benefit by that same generosity. Why can there not be more surfers who get seriously stoked when *other* surfers catch a good wave? Surfing ethics – that is, the ethics of surfers who relate to other surfers when surfing – is seldom given the column space it deserves in the surfing magazines.

The waves at Malpais' Playa Hermosa were pretty decent – solid five-foot sets (i.e. overhead faces) with some very fast 3-4 foot (head high) waves in between the sets. The break features a reef at the northern end where a legendary tubular right was not quite working, *and* a heavy right shoulder some eighty yards to the south of the reef, where half a dozen surfers were sitting. This shoulder was offering up a mix of close-outs and decent rides, which made the surfers cautious.

My friends paddled straight for the famous reef through the heaviest walls of whitewater, to try their luck where there might be tubes. I was eyeing that right shoulder, even though there was a small crowd on it. For one thing, my board was thicker than my buddies' boards (nearly 3"), being a brilliant 7'8" hybrid shaped by Rich Pavel from Ocean Beach, San Diego. This meant that the duck-diving through the heavy walls of whitewater would have overtired my then 56-year old shoulders. For another, I had already had my first open-heart surgery and was depending upon a pig valve, so there was some limitation in my ability to oxygenate my body.

In order to save some of my energy for the surfing, on the paddle-out I avoided the walls of whitewater at the reef and let myself drift southward to the next zone of heavy whitewater, emanating from the shoulder, thinking that my longer board would render me capable of making some of the sections that the younger surfers with shorter boards seemed to be unable to make. After another five minutes of heavy breathing, I pulled into the line-up, to be greeted with cold stares all around. No one was happy to see me.

These surfers had paid $2,000 for a month's rent of the only house around, which stood above the break about a ten-minute walk above the break. Much as the article described, after a week or so there they had already come to consider the break their territory, and I was not welcome. My point here is not to fault them, for in truth "they" are *us*. Why do we so quickly settle into territorial prerogatives, at the price of sacrificing even the most basic kindness we owe to strangers? My first thought was, "Hm. Pavones seems to be everywhere."

Just as soon as I finished that first thought, a set of right-breaking waves began heading toward us. Several surfers sitting to my left were too far beyond the breaking spot to catch it. One surfer to my immediate left thought he could catch it, but the first section of the wave closed out on him, so I took off and caught the shoulder just in the heart of the curl. After he disappeared in the whitewater, I made the turn and found the trim to ride a gem 60 or 70 yards across the shore. It had *plenty* of energy! I paddled back to the lineup from more or less where I had ended up, but again I drew nothing but hostile stares from the other surfers there too. I had gotten a good ride, which for some reason made me unpopular. Why do we not celebrate other people's good fortune? I didn't even dare to smile at them and only wondered where these people had learned their manners.

My friends had finally made it out right next to the reef, now even further away, leaving me a Lone Ranger for the moment, without any support. I felt that I could not even risk offering a "Hi" to the surfers that surrounded me. So since I had not really caught my breath after the paddle-out before that right had come to me, I just sat a bit outside the line-up, recovering.

But almost immediately an unexpected left-breaking wave I hadn't noticed before came directly toward me, and I was the only one who was in position for it. It was about two-thirds the size of the right I had just taken, but it was possibly even faster. It went for about 40 yards or so, leaving me to paddle out again pretty much where I had begun to ride the initial wave, but with the surfers there doubly pissed with me for having had two good rides in a row to their none. Why do we need to envy someone else's good fortune? It is a universal question, addressed by all of the major religions, which have not managed to have much success in transforming the human heart.

Especially, I wonder why it is that I myself cannot enjoy another surfer getting a good ride. Surfing is not really a zero-sum game; nevertheless, it can happen that one is gladdened when another surfer falls off a wave. Perhaps it makes us better by comparison, or it offers some consolation for having fallen off a ride ourselves. Celebrating others' good fortune is the bedrock of a Buddhist practice, but I seem to be too pathetic to practice it when I am surfing. That would be an accomplishment greater than riding a tube!

So I became caught up in the competitiveness of the moment, caught up in the social reality of these people who were definitely not Buddhists, and I became a willing co-conspirator, violating my own principles. I realized that now everyone in the small group around me was positively determined to catch the next wave in my stead. The proper way for me to have been thinking would have been, "Well, I just got two hot waves, let them have their turns now." But their vibes were so intense, so up-front and challenging, that I became sucked in. Especially intimidating was the gaze of a heavy-set, thickly tattooed blonde surfer dude sitting on his board to my immediate left, so much so that I was not inclined toward much generosity of spirit. Unlike myself, a serious practitioner of the path of a bodhisattva would have generously offered up the next wave anyway. Probably the brute was not really so bad after all. Instead, it was as the article about Pavones described it, "The energy at the peak is really negative. Everybody hates each other and wishes the worst." Including myself.

One of the three surfers who were closest to me took a small right and went down the line a short ways, a case of poor wave selection, leaving one surfer on either side of me. The tattooed dude was hanging close to my left, trying his best to intimidate me while retaining the full rights due to him as the likely outside-most rider. Most of all, he was determined that I would *not* get the next right-handed wave, or at least not another as good as the first one. He had become "agro" (aggressive). But he was sitting too far inside the shoulder, where the first section was still closing out. Moreover, the ocean's nearshore rip current was slowly moving both of us northward and had already moved him too far to be able to retain his outside post – he had been forced out of the sweet spot for the take-off spot for that wave.

The energy running between the two of us was sizzling. For a moment I thought of just paddling away to rejoin my friends, but there weren't any of those famous tubes breaking at the reef. So, since the waves at breaking at the reef were not very good, I remained there in the line-up, and I observed that in a minute or two I also would be moved by the current past the sweet spot; so I needed to take off on a wave very soon. Just then another set wave came, and it was going to close out badly. Mr. Tattoos, however, was so locked inside of the ignorance of his determination that I reckoned that he was going to take off on the wave no matter what. The reckoning of the affairs that were taking place there was subtle: I quickly calculated that Mr. Tatoos would paddle for it and then be forced to back off at the last moment, recognizing it was a no-go. This would leave him remaining next to me for the subsequent wave, with his anger even increased. How anathema this was to my Buddhist practice, but I was sucked into the ugliness of the moment: I decided to paddle for the wave too, acting as though I was going to steal the wave right in front of him, in order to coax his mind further inside his ignorance and distract him from inspecting too carefully the wave that was going to close out. This would make it more likely that he would actually take off into the inevitable wipe-out, thereby removing him from the lineup. Why was I so pathetically unable to eschew this kind of sadism that the situation provoked in me? *Please note*: anyone who wishes to encourage another person to remain engaged with his anger is *not* a Buddhist! I am a failure.

But the ploy worked. As soon as he saw me paddle for the wave, he geared himself tightly inside his decision to take off no matter what the wave might do. It was a solid five-foot wall and it closed out over him badly, completely dumping him and his board shoreward. That left only his friend, who was sitting inside me further down on the shoulder but with me now holding the outside rights. He would have to cede to me. This new development caused the remaining surfer to become seriously irritated with me.

A second but slightly smaller set wave came quickly, and its shape was much better than the previous wave. I was in the perfect position for it, but the friend on my inside made clear motions to indicate that this time he was going to cut me off and snag the wave for himself, regardless of the rules. And quite honestly, in light of the rule that says, "Never be a wave hog," he was not acting incorrectly. I should have backed off and let him have the wave, but his basic aggression was too blatant to allow my ego to permit him a victory.

I caught the wave in two strokes and rode higher up on the wave than usual, aiming my 7'8" board directly at the nose of the other surfer's board, daring him to try to drop in. For a moment he decided to do just that, and my ankle almost scraped the nose of his board, but he backed off, recognizing that I had too good of a position above him for him to do effective battle with me on that occasion. I slid past him, and it was a pretty decent ride.

Why does surfing have to be this way? Why did I participate in perpetuating this nonsense? How is it that we let ourselves keep becoming drawn into what stalls everyone's spiritual development? Further, does surfing assist or does it hinder one's spiritual development? By what skilled practices could even it be turned into the path? Is there something about the competitive individualism of surfing that lends itself to reinforcing the more indigent aspects of our character?

The practice here would be to resolve to be more generous in the water and thereby cultivate ways to offer other surfers some stoke about *their* rides. Pass up a wave from time to time, as a sort of spiritual exercise in disconnecting from one's avarice in the water (what Hindus and Buddhists call *aparigraha*, being content with less). Keep the broader picture in mind. Connect with sharing the experience with other surfers. That, as the authors from Surf-the-Planet suggest, is "the essence of surfing," to which I am blind despite all of my verbal heavy lifting.

Giving to others as a mere slogan has zero utility. Its efficacy consists only in the actual lived details. Resolve to foster good social vibes in the line-up, and let this work commence with just silently hoping that the other fellows catch good rides. It may not sound so difficult to the non-surfing reader, but silently hoping that each surfer always catches good waves is a challenging spiritual practice for a surfer to adopt. Radical. Converting the wish that others fall off to the wish that others get terrific rides is a simple yet effective means for improving one's character, one that is exercised where the real work of living is undertaken.

One day I will need to try it.

37
Cultivating Distractions

Frank was worn much beyond his 59 years. His schizophrenia had burned out too many of his synapses. While he had preserved his innate sense of revelry, he was distracted continually by his own ceaseless fretting. I had accompanied his brother, who had gone to visit him one Sunday where he lived, a home for mental patients, and we took him to a nearby arboretum that afforded excellent views of the environs. He was grateful for his brother's visit, kissing him and telling him, "You never forget me!"

As we drove to the arboretum, we sang some songs together. When they were teenagers, the two of them had had a band; in fact, Frank was still a brilliant pianist. Although his spirits were high, he was unable to settle into any peace that could endure longer than a few seconds. After we arrived at the arboretum, a field of pines was somehow disconcerting to him: "Let's go. We need to get going. Let's not dally!" he told us, even though he had no place to go except back to the home for the mental patients. When we stopped to gaze at a monument for a moment, his impatience overwhelmed him: "We don't have the time to be dilly-dallying like this. Let's move on!"

I recognized the sentiment. When I make the long I-5 drive from Oregon to Baja California, I find it almost impossible to stop. The urge to keep moving propels me for its own sake, since the velocity of movement dictates its own temporality. It offers an illusion of progress, even when it is empty of content – it is almost the iconic form of American progress. Highway 66! While contemplating the face of my friend's brother, I was able to consider having devoted a good deal of my own life, perhaps the majority of it, hurrying to get nowhere. Where is it that we think we are heading that will so fabulously be capable of resolving our anxieties and doubts? What is it that is embedded deeply within human habits that keeps causing us to defer our repose for some deferred state of perfection that is only imagined – like freedom itself – and exists more in its anticipation than in actual experience? We are masters of producing distractions, and we cultivate these distractions as if we were addicts. Schizophrenics are excellent at offering us exaggerated versions of our own shortcomings.

Were Frank to stop for a moment to fully inhabit a single moment, he might recognize that what he was anticipating with his infinite deferrals was already present. How unfortunate it is to be blind to the solution that is already within one!

Frank is not so very different from the rest of us. He only presents us with a more obvious case of our own dementia, thereby affording us an opportunity to examine ourselves. What makes the case of Frank so laden with significance for me is that these brothers are actually my second cousins, living in Italy. Frank does not speak a word of English, but he looks more like me than any other person who lives on this earth, including my own brother. This greatly enhanced the pertinence of the illustration for me, making it almost scary.

The business of modernity is distraction, and it has arrived in our present moment of cultural evolution (which is always species evolution too) like a flood. No one seems able to afford the time to recognize what they possess already, and the imagined urgency of their efforts leads them to search for it everywhere, except where it is actually to be found. As the Panchen Lama says, "You are like the one who keeps surveying the landscape everywhere in search of the very donkey on which you are riding."

38
A Compassion That Respected Marriage

He was a bright and educated Tibetan, just approaching middle-age. His wife was an even brighter Tibetan woman, but she had aged more quickly than he. His task was to serve as communicator and facilitator between some Western Buddhist students and their Tibetan teachers during a week-long course. They were childless, and an unhappiness shadowed their personalities.

The American student was a bright, educated middle-aged woman. Though articulate and quick-witted, her plainness had worked against her, leaving her without a mate. Her loneliness was like a companion, and it accompanied her spirit wherever she went.

There are so many unhappy people.

The American woman went to the Tibetan man's door to ask about the roommate she was assigned for the week, but when their eyes met there was an instantaneous but silent communication, and she could only stumble over her request. He didn't catch the meaning of her words, but he did grasp the more vital and pertinent communication that was at work.

He visited her room many times over the next several days, and they pruned for each other morning, noon, and night. A new energy leapt into their spirit. Their discussions were full of words, but it was the physical character of the sounds that captivated them more than the meanings. Clearly, romance was afoot.

On the third day she met his wife (who was ignorant of their brewing relations), and the American woman examined her carefully. She easily recognized an honest, decent woman who was bearing a recognizable sadness, and she felt compassion for her.

The courtship continued for a few more days, as the American assessed, considered, and reassessed her situation. How could she measure her own sadness against the sadness of this other woman? How realistic was this budding love that her suitor bore earnestly? Even more, were human yearnings ever capable of being satisfied? What was love and what was infatuation, and how does one tell them apart (if one can)?

After more deliberation, and considering that the damage to be done was more certain than the endurance of the romance, she concluded it was wrong to act upon her heartache and thereby complicate the already difficult life of an honest woman. She was uncomfortable with the idea of being the vehicle for such a tragedy, and so she departed the retreat center quietly before the week's program was completed. He was broken-hearted, although he was not unmindful of the wisdom of her decision, which only made his feeling for her burn more strongly.

I'm no expert in such matters, but it seems to me likely that it was an infatuation that might have relieved them of their loneliness for a short while but was unlikely to transform their lives in a durable way; it was more hope than solution. Naturally, marriage may be much the same. But life is quite finite, and perhaps we should resolve the karma of our present circumstances before heaping new karma upon it, even though all three concluded the week with their sadness undiminished.

39
Obsolete in My Own Time

The easiest route to mental health lies in simplifying one's daily life. Then one can tap the abundant supply of silence that exists in the cosmos. That silence is the best ally one has, and it is always available for nourishing our sanity. Unfortunately, modern life consists mostly of noise and distractions that crowd out the silence. What is more astonishing is that we mostly mistake the distractions for happiness.

Distractions include the following situations:

(1) Our televisions now broadcast hundreds of channels and even offer us the possibility of displaying multiple stations on the same screen, including programs that were recorded previously, so that even when we are watching a program that fits our interest, we can be jarred constantly by visions of other potential viewings that might even be more satisfying. Even if one is able to win the battle over the remote control, one does not have the time to review everything that is available for viewing. It may be possible to follow intelligently two or three programs simultaneously, but why would one *want* to do that? I do not keep any television myself, and I have not kept one for 40 out of the last 42 years. When I arrive at a friend's home and find myself in the mood to take a peak at contemporary culture, I find that I no longer have the technological prowess to even turn the thing on successfully. First, there is always a pile of remote controls, sometimes in a grass basket or large clay bowl, and I have difficulty discerning which one is the gadget that actually operates the television. Frequently the battery is dead (since I may have been allocated a

spare room); sometimes one remote operates the sound, another the satellite dish, and a third the channel selection. Determining which are the working remotes among a bowl-full of remotes can be an impossible task, so my attempts to watch television are mostly stillborn, and I am thrust back into that silence that is the default state of the universe.

People ask me, "Don't you miss what is truly worth watching on television?" I reply by explaining that I do not doubt that there is excellent viewing available on television. It is just that the television fills up all of the space in the house, crowding out one's own thoughts! No matter how good it may be, television is suffocating: it steals one's soul. Consider the empty feeling that usually follows a period of many hours of television viewing. I was among the first humans to grow up with a television in every room of the house (my father manufactured televisions), so it is not that I have no experience with the phenomenon. I will grant that television can be very good; but my own thoughts can be even better, especially when I am is able to sustain their *continuity* without continual interruptions.

(2) Everywhere advertising billboards clamor for our attention. I don't just mean the static billboards of the past that were found alongside the roadways throughout America, and which were scars on any landscape; instead, I mean billboards that flash, blink, and spin in full video color. Flashing what? Usually something designed to arouse one sexually (otherwise, it would be difficult to get a person to surrender the priority that is rightfully due to driving the car). Billboards now do everything except jump up into the sky and perform summersaults; in fact, a few of them seem to do that as well, but they are only illusions. Sometimes entire buildings are wrapped in attractive HD advertising gauze, and they are so huge that it is impossible to avoid them.

The late Geshe Rabten, a leading Sera lama from the middle of the last century, once advised me that when I returned to the US I should endeavor to keep my eyes trained to the ground in order to avoid the many skilled techniques being used to attract my mind. But a sign the size of a thirty-story building that is dancing in one's face is nearly impossible to avoid. These video-billboards are not only placed along highways, there are also screens located on the front of the gas pumps that play while one is pumping gas! They are also in most taxis throughout the world; in fact, one cannot any longer look out of most taxi windows since there is always a video advert in one's face, and one's only recourse is to throw one's sweater over the display as best one can. There are even video-boards in some urinals at gas stations, so one cannot even urinate without having more advertisements shoved in front of one's face. If a man could only raise one leg like a Great Dane and pee on the video-board in protest! Being distracted by billboards has become so second nature that most people think I am the one who is unreasonable for bothering to complain. The judgment is clear: I have become obsolete in my own time.

There is some reason for optimism on this point, however. São Paolo, Brazil, has not only banned *all* billboards in that city, *no building* (other than major tourist hotels) *is permitted to erect an electrified sign!* With 20 million people, São Paolo is one of the hugest cities in the world, yet it offers its citizens a distraction free environment; moreover, its residents love the policy. The sign-free horizon of that city was for me the most remarkable thing about Brazil, since it constitutes a frontal assault upon consumerism. It is much more radical in undermining capitalist culture than anything that a communist nation has devised.

(3) We are now distracted not by only the usual meaningless magazines and newspapers on supermarket counters that reshuffle the same scandals in different arrangements, today we can easily be overwhelmed by the way that one's computer collects them all as podcasts, tweets, Facebook messages, etc. In addition, there are the daily emails that I attend to as a solemn duty to my friends

and colleagues. I cannot imagine taking on the additional *daily* responsibility to cover more institutionalized communication, such as checking a second email account, maintaining one or more Facebook identities, engaging in Twitter communication, PayPal, Amazon, Craigslist, etc., for such regular effort would leave me without much discretionary time for more productive pursuits, pursuits that generally require some silence.

In recent years I have noticed while backpacking in the high granite mountains of California that the choicest lakes that once were too crowded to consider for camping are now vacant, even during the peak weeks of the summer: my own generation has become too elderly and frail to carry a backpack and the nation's present youth do not dare leave their internet identities unattended for the week it takes to reach and return from the better lakes.

(4) Telephones: I don't mean making or receiving a phone call, I mean devices that have become the natural extension of one's nervous system. It was 25 years ago that I removed the telephone from my home, for the reason that I was constantly hounded by (a) telemarketers that seemed to call only while I was eating dinner, and (b) dozens of students who were selfishly trying to pump me for which questions were likely to appear on the next test. Changing or delisting my phone number was insufficient, since both of the above groups were able to quickly relocate my number. So I removed the phone from my house altogether, leaving my office phone the only way to reach me. What I did not expect was how wonderfully nurturing was the silence that ensued after I had discarded the phone. That became a real treasure, and so I have adhered to my policy ever since.

The capacity to embrace silence is not widespread. There is a kind of emptiness that appears whenever the interstices of our daily lives are exposed (the first day of summer vacation, the day after graduation, the month following the completion of a book, etc.). One somehow needs continual reassurance from one's work, or friends and associates, that one's identity is real, and without that reassurance one can grow anxious. The problem we are faced with as human beings is that one's identity is *not* real! Not at all.

The only thing that is real is the primordial, living mind that pre-existed our identity and whose vibrations are too subtle to detect underneath all of the noisy distractions that we have piled on top of it. Connecting with that original mind is our most important work as human beings. The Australian Aboriginal people I lived with for two years were always in touch with it, on a daily basis, but we supposedly more advanced people have lost our connections with what Heidegger has called "our ownmost being."

Finally, there are the cell phones, the principal subject of this reflection. They are all of the above on steroids. The iPhone is to the old landline that I removed from my home what a million-pixeled video billboard is to the roadway sign of the 1950s. It does everything: it locates what constellation one is looking at; it provides a photo of the street along which one is walking; and it plays one's favorite music and videos, and features your beloved ones live in front of your face, anytime. I have been to concerts, even classical ones, where members of the audience preferred to witness the evening's performance through the tiny screen of their cell phone as they recorded it. These phones are too marvelous, and that is their problem! They are so marvelous that one is too ready and willing to sacrifice the silence that is our real heritage.

When cell phones first appeared, I thought that they might be worth trying out. But right away I witnessed people taking calls as though each time their personal ringtone went off, it was providing public evidence of their personal importance, popularity, and indispensability. This only encouraged them to commence their conversation using a volume that was always louder than normal speech, even in elevators, buses, restaurants, and other public places. The people who used cell phones were so obnoxious that at once I resolved never to get one. It seemed only to reinforce one of the worst characteristics of humans, their self-absorption. The philosopher Emmanuel Levinas has exhorted us to listen to the Other, to remain open to the call to responsibility elicited by the look that emanates from the eyes of another person we see. I wondered, how will people be able to answer the call of that look, when they never notice anything beyond their ear buds? Think of the people who are listening only to the music in their ears, oblivious to anyone else; they are not prepared to be social beings.

One of my favorite illustrations of karma is when two cyclists in Eugene became so lost inside of their earphone-rendered symphonies that they collided head-on with each other. Each of them blamed the other. Students walk out into the middle of busy streets wearing Bose headphones while staring at the text messages on their iPhone screen; hearing nothing and seeing nothing, it is amazing that.more are not run over. Our society is heading for troubles, and it is a nightmare that is international. My taxi driver in Istanbul or Bangalore is more clued in to modern life than I am.

If I was a young person I would get a cell phone since it has become a part of being in society, but that does not negate the fact that some people have lost the ability to say hello, which is not very social either. Cashiers in America wish to scan your item, collect your money, and provide you your change without ever making eye contact. Having spent much time in Italy in recent years, I have noticed that they have not yet reached this point; in fact, there the lines move at a snail's pace, and the server frequently wishes to chat with each customer about personal aspects of their lives. It is really wonderfully human, although it drives crazy any visiting Swiss who are waiting in line. There is no longer much of this kind of civility in the world. In a study I made at my university, students from Japan, China, and Korea reported their conclusion that the American greeting ("Hi!" – "Hi!") was shallow and that Americans did not seem to know what real friendship was. The Japanese and Chinese may dislike each other, but they were in complete agreement regarding the shallowness of the customary relations displayed on American streets. The cell phone has made these matters worse, including making it easier for the Japanese and Chinese to share our practices.

The other day I was walking along a lane at Sera Monastery in South India, where I was spending the season, and I passed an older Tibetan geshe (professor) in his robes who I had never seen before who was walking along the same lane, so I greeted him "Tashi Delek!" which means literally, "May you have happiness and good fortune." But I offered it in a perfunctory tone, much in the mechanical way that Americans make most of their greetings (i.e., "Hi!" – "Hi!"). The geshe at once asked me, in Tibetan, "Do you know what is the meaning of 'Tashi Delek'?" He wished to teach me that one could use the opportunity of making such a greeting for the purpose of cultivating in one's heart a genuine wish that the other person may find happiness, and that if one ignored the opportunity to cultivate such a sentiment, one was losing a ready-made opportunity to practice Buddhism. I replied in Tibetan, "Yes, I do. It means that one generates in one's heart a hope that the other person experiences some happiness. Thank you, Geshe-la." He was pleased that I recognized my dharmic mistake at once, without him having to do much explanation. He was sharp to notice that my greeting was lacking in sincerity: he had caught me red-handed.

My mindlessness is nothing in comparison with the bubbles of self-absorption that are wandering the streets of the world today, oriented primarily to their cell phones. My students move through the world cell phone-first. Observe outside the door of any classroom as it opens: whether the class is in session or has just ended, in most cases the first thing you will see after the door opens is a cell phone, followed by a hand, then an arm, and at last a person. The same is true for elevators: as the doors open, the people exit with their cell phones first, in a pose that resembles the

Statue of Liberty. Sometimes they have been so engrossed in their text message that they miss their floor, and so they head straight for the stairwell so that they can climb the stairs back down to the floor they passed while they were absorbed with their cell phone.

These humans' lives are largely confined to the bubble of concern that emanates from their cell phone, and they are not well prepared for much live relating with the people with whom they share social space. They don't seem to really care about those people. They may not even *see* those people; they may not even wish to see those people. The problem is that those people interfere with their self-absorption, and they become offended by the interference. I am reminded of a Tibetan commentary, "People are attached to their selfish preoccupations and to their personal sphere of relations." Heidegger says that people are "caught up" for the most part with whatever is most proximal – with whatever is immanent, right in front of them, closest to their faces. And today what is closest is one's cell phone, and this too frequently prevents other people from making genuine contact with them. They are unable to free themselves up from their mundane distractions enough to witness the being that is just beneath their noses. This sounds like metaphysics, but it's really a practical observation.

Most of my students are no longer able to pay attention to a lecture, since they must continually monitor their cell phone for that text message-in-the-sky, the one that when it arrives is going to transform their lives and provide them with endless happiness. You see them checking their phones and frowning when they realize that the message that signaled was not the one they were anticipating. Even when they are diligent in their attempt to listen to the lecture and they ignore checking to see what the text message that arrived could be, their internal musing about which text message it might be prevents them from really hearing the lecture. Some of the students seem to have not concentrated seriously for years, so acclimatized are they to this cavalcade of electronic distractions. When they visit me in my office and their phone ringtone goes off, they answer the call ("I'll just take this one") and expect me to wait while they finish their urgent business. For this reason, I first make them turn the phones off and put them in their bags; a request that sometimes offends them. Even then some students speak to me while texting on their left bare palm with their right index finger, without a phone, spelling out on their palms the words that are most important in whatever they are telling me. All of this has reinforced my decision not to become caught up with the cell phone culture.

Recently a young Tibetan *rinpoche* (a reincarnated lama) expressed to me the view that we had an obligation to use cell phones in order to make us available to our friends and other associates who may have some need of us. He expressed the opinion that not having a cell phone was a form of selfishness. He may be right. I have received as presents new cell phones from both my brother and my son, so that they would be able to reach me more easily, but both of these phones remain in their original packaging in one of my drawers at home. I cannot even tell you which drawer, and in any case they are now probably too old to function with any existing system. Do I have an obligation to make myself constantly available to friends who wish to contact me? The system I have now is that anyone who wishes to speak with me sends me an email, and I 'Skype' them. The advantage of this is that the procedure is cumbersome enough that I am able to avoid 99% of calls this way. So perhaps it is selfish, my own variety of self-absorption.

My friends tell me that I can always keep a cell phone turned off until I choose to receive calls. My problem is that if that is the case the phone would be off nearly all of the year, and there would be little point in my paying for the service. But perhaps the problem is really not that – I am deterred by the likely possibility that I will prove incapable of keeping it turned off. The danger is that my own cell phone use will creep inside of my nervous system until it takes over completely, and before long the silence that is one's natural and best task master will no longer be available in the same abundance. That is my fear. There seems to be no such thing as judicious use of a cell phone, and at least for me the real choice seems to be between using it like an addict or not using one at all. I can learn from my relation with my emails that I probably would not have enough strength of character to remain in control of the situation.

Some friends and neighbors think I'm a lunatic for this, and others (possibly the majority) think I am just joking with them when I tell them I do not have a cell phone. Still others think I am being dishonest about it, imagining that I do not like them enough to give them my number. If I explain that I have no telephone of any kind, they treat me as if I was a derelict. The 90 year-old mother of one of my best Indian friends, a friend for whom I helped find a visa and some employment for a season in the US, noticed that I had no cell phone, and she told her son, "I don't see how he can be a very important person – he owns no cell phone and does not even wear a wristwatch!" Well, she's right about my not being an important person.

Moreover, if the truth is told one of the most powerful reasons that motivate my not having a cell phone is a stubborn anti-establishmentarianism that operates at the core of my self-identity, so this too is an ego trip for me. My favorite boasts are that I do not own a television nor go to movies, despite my being born in Hollywood. I have not seen Star Wars or Star Trek and cannot tell the two apart. I once had a meal at a lunch counter in Hollywood and began talking with the person who was sitting next to me. This person seemed surprised that I did not recognize who he was, and from that I deduced that he must be a famous movie star (having grown up there, I instantly recognized the interactional components that indicate this). We spoke about a number of topics, and all the while he was checking carefully to see if it was really true that I did not recognize him. Once he became certain that I had no idea who he was, he wanted to become my good friend. He asked me where I was from, probably thinking I was from North Dakota or Oklahoma; when I replied, "I was born about half a mile from here," he practically fell off of his lunch stool. I reflected afterward that while I never had the ambition to become a Hollywood star – I grew up with many of their children, and so I knew well that it is not a life to be sought or envied – I was unable to avoid cultivating some egotism about not caring about Hollywood stars; so egotism has won out in the end, as it usually will.

Not long ago, I was trying to make a call from my office phone at the university, and I reached a wrong number. I politely asked the young man who received the errant call to tell me what number I reached, since I wished to know whether I had dialed the number that was on my piece of paper correctly and thereby avoid disturbing him twice. He said, "Just look at your cell phone, you'll find the number there." I replied, and I think it was another of my boasts, "I'm not using a cell phone; I don't even own a cell phone." His response: "Boy, you really are a loser then," and he hung up. Rather than taking his judgment seriously, it only enhanced my pride that I have managed to live contentedly outside the limits of what some people accept to be universal. It makes me feel special; like never having made a purchase at Walmart, or ever having eaten a hamburger at Macdonalds, or had an ice cream or a Coca-Cola during the last 45 years. By convincing me that I am unique, they are every one of them ego trips.

So is my resistance to getting a cell phone just another ego trip? Do I have an obligation to be contactable? Even, is my life becoming too isolated this way? Or worse, "Am I missing out?" Et cetera. I don't think I'm missing out on anything except becoming more distracted, but I am challenged to think beyond my practice of not using cell phones by a monk addicted to a cell phone who grew up in a Buddhist monastery!

Yes, the monks in the Tibetan monastery express incredulity upon learning that they cannot contact me by cell phone. They too may think I must be a loser. I noticed that the young monks who memorize their texts in the evenings do so now with their cell phones lit up, and I am sure that it must make their work of memorization more difficult. Perhaps it trains them to be good at multitasking. I do hope they turn off their cell phones at least while they meditate, but they probably do not always do so, right?! The distractions of cell phones may undo some of the ability to concentrate with single-minded focus, which is preliminary to calm abiding and is one of the historic pillars of the practice of Buddhism. I certainly see many of the lamas, both high and low, who seem to be appended to their cell phones in the same way that my students are.

For the present, I am swayed by two practical matters: first, neither of my two homes in North America – my cabin in a wilderness area of northern California and my beach house in Baja California nestled inside of some sand dunes that block cell phone reception – is capable of receiving any signals; second, at my now advanced age my eyesight is not good enough to spend all of the day squinting at a 3" x 2" screen, even with my reading glasses. Simply the thought of doing so is painful to me. I know, I know, my son has already informed me that now they have iPads that are "large enough to land an airplane on." I prefer to wait until iPads become obsolete like me, which cannot be so very long now.

Of one thing I am certain: silence will never become obsolete.

V

Concluding Stories

40
Stopping the World in the Era of Multitasking

Sometimes I find myself grinning in the morning as I sit with my early morning coffee, reading a book at my desk while the winter sun shines squarely on my lap through my study window. Things worked out well in my study, which I built more than 20 years ago. In the wintertime, the dawning sun rousts my brain into early action, and its warmth is even more welcome when the morning airs are in the 40s. In the summertime, when I do not require additional heat, the sun rises too far in the northeast to strike my study window directly until it has risen too high to be able to cast its rays inside the room.

I'm not certain what it is that makes me so happy early in the morning, since little has yet happened in the day; there is just an overwhelming wave of contentment to which I surrender. Perhaps these interstices of our lives – the silences between the more "important" things – are where we really live and where we have the most access to the innate being that underlies all of our identity-creating activities. One cannot plan for them, though, they have to fall into one's lap as it were, just as this late December early morning sunshine is doing now. One does have to be prepared to notice it, however, which is something for which we do not always have the time. In this way we become our own enemy – we make ourselves too busy to stop to notice. Even our meditation sessions become more busyness.

Oddly, my book-reading seems to help, although which particular book it is that I am reading has little bearing on matters. The reading only provides a conduit for my body's energy, which cycles from the pages of the book to my solar plexus, up my spine to my brain, and back down to the book again. The reading provides a place for the mentation of my consciousness to settle, where it can be tamed, and in this work the yoga of reading is itself more important than the subjects I am reading about. Perhaps years ago the topics were more important for me, but after so many books it hardly matters any more. I don't really need to read another book; I have read so many of them, what all-important difference could another one make? But the physical action, the yoga of the act itself – sitting in my chair and channeling my nervous energy into a book, steadying it and calming myself is what counts. The longer I sit reading, the more calm I become. After several hours, the contentment can grow into something fabulous. It can be given the name bliss.

While this experience is a daily possibility, it is more usual for my contentment to be thrown off of its tracks by some intervening anxiety or "rush," that is, by a faster movement of mentation that intervenes as soon as I recall that I am facing some new deadline or have forgotten some urgent task – an article that is overdue at the editor's or the grant application that has to be finished by next month that I recall only *just now* as I write these very words on this page. Darn! The internet has increased these interruptions seven-fold, since all that one needs is a single email or Skype call to throw one out of one's calm centering for the rest of the week, morning sun or no morning sun. This is why I keep my computer off the first hour each morning as the Baja sun glances softly through my window onto my lap. The human mind may not be basically restless, but so much restlessness is heaped atop it that only rarely are we able to clear this restlessness off the decks. It is not so frequently that we are open to the underlying peace that is resting here all the while, unnoticed.

Two decades ago this region of Baja California Norte, Mexico, experienced its hundred-year flood. While there are few domiciles in this mostly forgotten desert, the floods took out the highway bridges over the arroyos (dry river beds) both north and south of me. The result was that for two weeks no one could go anywhere, nor was there any electricity since many of the electric poles were washed away. But I was able to keep surfing, on a new sand bar that the flooding arroyo had formed, because there is no power capable of shutting off the ocean's constant pulsations to which I keep myself closely attuned. It was the best two weeks of my life, with no close second. The quiet was immaculate, and it put all of my neighbors into a good mood. There were no interruptions. Like coming home at last, I had only the vibrations of my own thought for keeping me company. *The world had stopped*, and peace flooded in to occupy the space that was vacated.

Why can we not institute such wholesale peace on our own? And do so anytime that we desire it? My capacity to distract myself astonishes me. Now that I am finally retired, there are no more committees, no reports or paper grading, nor do I need to commit to any deadlines that I don't volunteer for. So why do I volunteer for them, to the point of my becoming stressed by them like before? Do I need them because my life has become too empty without those deadlines? It can be frightening as well as liberating. Do I deliberately add a few deadlines to give my life some structure, or purpose, or distractions? Am I addicted to distractions? What are these rushed senses of things that "have to be done" that sweep over me and keep encumbering the wholesale peace to which I have found my way? Why am I mostly powerless to ignore them?

For example, it so happens that just now I am writing five books, and I am in love with each one of them. But that is a recipe for schizophrenia, not the peace of the *vanasthāna* (the period of life when one enters the forest in order to learn what it will take to be able to die meaningfully). My principal aim is to write each book slowly, without "fastness" or restlessness, so that I can use the writings to cultivate my *samādhi* (*sama* = same; *dhi* =

mental comportment) and retain the stability of the quiet peace that the silence of my residence here affords. But despite this aim, I find myself stressing myself about getting each next chapter completed in a timely way, and by the writings I have had to leave aside. I am confronted with this question: if I now have all the time in the world, along with the most nurturing projects imaginable, why am I incapable of just settling peacefully into my work and instead battle weekly with the breathlessness introduced by my having too many projects to complete?

The problem is that my life is too much of a good thing. On occasion I reflect that just the reading of the background books for all five of my writing projects will take me more years than I have left in my now elderly life. I will have to stop reading at least some of them soon. As one of my precious teachers, a Vedanta master and chemistry professor from Bangalore by the name of Satyanarayana Shastry once advised me long ago, "Ken, you do realize, don't you, that one day you will have to abandon all your eager questing and learn to be content with whatever you have managed to find?" Could that day have arrived? When it does will I ever have the spiritual strength to recognize it and to permit myself to simply be?

Part of the sense of peace in my morning studio is the bookshelves of topics there that are the residues of my many journeys and that contain the rich source materials for my many quests. These bookshelves are an environment of possibilities that reflect in physical form my own imaginings: postmodern inquiries into the productive uses of logic and reason, Tibetan Buddhist investigations of something similar, paleoarcheological examinations of the frail and brief history of hominids, a shelf of six different translations of the *Yoga Vasistha* (my favorite book), five shelves of contemporary poetry (the only bookshelves I allow into my living room), two shelves about native edible plants (a lifetime hobby), et cetera. These very collections that nurture me also stare down at me as indictments, in the form of the many volumes among them that remain unread.

I am reminded of the spring break I took in Oregon following an especially hard winter term of teaching when I had more than 600 students in two large lecture classes. During that term I had no time to read my *New Yorker* magazines, which kept arriving weekly and were stacked up, one on top of the other, on a corner of my desk. The quality of the writing in the *New Yorker* is so excellent that I wanted to read them all, so I took them (about a dozen issues) to my beach house along the Oregon coast and spent the entire spring break reading them. When on the concluding Sunday I finally finished with the last issue, I had a peculiar sense of accomplishment – as in, "There, now that one is done!" And so I could check that item off of my written list of things that needed doing. Such lists can help us accomplish things, but those lists also hound us, alienating us from ourselves. I observed the triviality of my sense of satisfaction in having finally cleared my desk of those *New Yorker* magazines that were indicting me for my inattention, and I cried out loud, "What idiocy!" I cancelled my subscription, as well as my subscription to all my magazines (except one, *Yoga Life*), and I have been free of them ever since.

About the same time I had another epiphany. I observed that about mid-morning each day I would begin to tune into the possibility of the mailman's arrival. Nearly each day at 11 am, he or she would arrive at the rural mailbox of my isolated Oregon beach home with a stack of letters for me. On some days those letters were my sole contact with the outside world. Several days in a row I noticed myself gearing up for "that time" even though usually nothing more significant arrived than bills and advertisements. Thinking about it as a phenomenon, I noticed that my anticipation of the mail each day was distracting me from whatever I was doing at my desk. I was giving force to the illusion that real happiness was something that was still to come, perhaps in the day's mail. My anticipation was far out of proportion to its real worth. So I took drastic action: I cut down the post that held up my mailbox and filed a forwarding notification at the post office, using my office at the university as the forwarding address. From then on, there was no mail and no mailpersons, leaving me much more opportunity to cultivate my own concentrations.

Last year I managed the extraordinary feat of checking for mail at my San Diego mailbox at the post office only six times during the year. I checked it once in late January, prior to leaving for a teaching assignment in China. The next time was in September when I arrived back in San Diego for my trip back to my home in Baja California. I have no other mailing address than that post office, and so I received mail only six times in the entire year. This year I checked it four times. Since I can detect a trend here, I suppose I have been successful with minimizing at least this one distraction.

An important discipline to learn is to resist and pacify the force of any restless energy that threatens to overtake one's mental stream. That is practically the only secret one needs to learn. Consequently, one needs to be mindful about when writing books too, for like anything they can become distractions.

In graduate school I knew a fellow Phd. student, Carlos Castaneda, who shared the same professor-mentor that I had. Castaneda was fond of talking about "stopping the world," by which he meant this bringing the fastness of one's living to a halt so that one could "be" instead of always becoming swept away by "doing" things. When one stopped the world, there was ample opportunity for the natural quiet of existence to assert itself, silencing the distractions to which we have given ourselves. Castaneda even later devoted a large part of his third book, *Journey to Ixtlan*, to a section that was titled, "Stopping the World," which also contained chapters on "Erasing Personal History," "Losing Self-Importance," "Death as an Adviser," "Disrupting the Routines of Life," and "Not Doing," etc., all of which sound like they could have been taken from any textbook on Buddhism. The idea is that until one learns how to resist and pacify the fast notions that enter our hearts and carry away our minds, one will never find enduring peace. This is primarily a practical matter, not a theoretical one.

Instead of learning how to silence our busy minds, our life sometimes consists of cultivating new ways to enhance the distractions! When conversing with my son a month back, he carried out an hour-long conversation with me while he was surfing on the internet. In fact, his laptop, iPad, or cell phone (or all these) is never very far away from him, and I think the world-wide-web has become a natural extension of his nervous system, in much the same way that the white cane of a blind man becomes part of a blind person's body. When I suggested to my son that he should give me his undivided attention, he replied, "Don't worry, Dad, I'm really good at multi-tasking."

I will grant that the metabolic economy of the nervous system of a young man may well benefit from finding outlets for the abundant nervous energy and hormones that sweep through a young person's body, perhaps in the way that I use reading books in the mornings. But I cannot believe that the essentially self-distracting nature of internet surfing – during which one not infrequently finds oneself having completely *forgotten* about the search that led one into the web in the first place – is the sort of mental practice that one wants to become conditioned to. Cell phone intrusions have no relief either. In fact, it can be the case that when there are no such intrusions one feels empty!

An alternative is to find ways to reassert the natural flow of non-distraction. In fact, this is what is meant by Patañjali's notion of *pratyahara*, one of the eight limbs of classical yoga, although it is the limb that people overlook and contemplate the least since few understand it and even fewer are able to practice it. Some Western practitioners of yoga fear it as a severe form of self-denial.

Frequently it is translated as "abstinence" or "sensory withdrawal," something that can really frighten Americans, but that does not really approach its meaning. *Pratyahara* is the process of coming to rely – on an habitual basis – upon inner resources for feeling satisfied, instead of depending upon less reliable external sources of pleasure. It is all about satisfaction and contentment. Probably many if not most people are frightened away by the sense of emptiness that a lack of distraction may leave them with, and so they fear to stop the world, but it is possible to solicit that emptiness and even to find nurture in it: "You *can* do!" as Lama Yeshe used to say.

The master course of dharma practice consists of sticking with what is simple and proximate – the pacification of present being, or "stopping the world" – resisting the way that one's attentions and energy flow outwards to whatever distraction newly presents itself, like water seeking the lowest ground. This practice of dharma can work only when one turns off the tap, cold turkey. The good news is that each instant offers another opportunity to try this out.

Here is one way to give oneself an edge in beginning this practice. It is a simple non-exercise: in a comfortable place (preferably outdoors) lie on your stomach and relax. If the ground is unclean, use a mat or rug. Stretch your legs out straight and rest the tops of your feet on the ground, stomach touching the ground with the soles of your feet facing upward. Place one hand over the other, the palms of your hands facing down, while your elbows and forearms remain in contact with the ground. Lower your neck and place your chin comfortably on the back of your hands, while you breathe slowly. Then let go – just relax, breathing slowly. After a short time you will find that the restlessness of your mind will cease by itself, and an utter peace will take up residence inside your spine. It is something about the nerves' flow in this position that relaxes one, and as long as one is resting in this position, the world will simply pass one by. A variation of this practice that is equally powerful is to place the arms underneath the legs, with the backs of the hands touching the ground between the ground and the front of the quadriceps, the palms making contact with the quadriceps while resting one's chin directly on the ground. I find this to be a primordial, even embryonic, position, conducive for letting go of mental tension. The greater the worries and concerns you have, the more effective this non-exercise for stopping the world will be. It always works.

The more important practice is to learn how to wake up and undertake the daily tasks of your life with a calmness and lack of frenzy. Make each task a portion of one's *sādhaṇā* (daily practice). For myself, this means that when I turn to my book projects I try to pursue each thread of reflection and exploration as an opportunity to practice how to think without haste. It is a matter of self-control, and we *can* control our hearts. Even when the notes for my book (which are now lying all over my desk on different colored papers, and in colored inks) defy my organizing, and my work becomes like herding cats, I celebrate this newly arrived opportunity for me to practice cultivating a calm mind as I cope with the chaos.

41
The Four Noble Truths

The first time I heard about The Four Noble Truths was when I read a chapter devoted to India in my seventh grade geography class textbook. I was only twelve years old, a boy growing up in Beverly Hills, and at that time I had taken my life there for a normal one, mostly unaware that I was living in one of the most affluent economic environments in the world. Still, it was my version of ordinary. I never considered my family especially rich, but that was because I compared myself to the families of my friends (our maid only came twice a week while my friends' maids lived in, and our swimming pool was smaller). I had a wonderful time growing up there – the schools were great, the sports were great, and the food was great. Life was fun, the way it should be for a kid.

The authors of my geography textbook had placed their presentation of "The Four Noble Truths" in an insert box at the bottom of a page in their chapter on "India," and I remember being stunned to read and consider the Truths: Suffering is all pervading; suffering has a Cause, which is desire; that cause has a remedy, which is the Cessation of desire; and that cessation can be achieved by effective Practice. I did a kind of double-take: what was all of this preoccupation with suffering? I thought to myself, "My goodness, those poor people living over in India must be having a very difficult time if they think all of life is suffering!" That was not a "truth" I was expecting to hear. I considered that they had a distorted perspective due to all of the disease and poverty they must have. The largest dilemma that I had to face was deciding which of the 31 flavors I would choose at the Baskin-Robbins ice cream parlor on our twice-weekly trip for double cones. On the Saturday after I read about The Four Noble Truths, I spent part of the day wondering where was all of this suffering that these Buddhists mentioned, as I walked the two blocks from my house to Roxbury Park with my football under my arm, singing the latest rock-and-roll song (it was "Rockin' Robin"). My life was so filled with what was fun, how could I possibly measure of the truth of suffering? I resolved that it would probably be best if I avoided ever going to India, and I felt quite sorry for them.

As things turned out, I ended up spending much of my life in India (I have lived there more than six years, and I am in my 60s); in fact, I consider it to be as much my home as Baja California Norte, Los Angeles, or Oregon. That is not the only irony that life has thrown into my path. I recall the first time I visited Eugene, Oregon, on my way to a backpacking expedition in the North Cascades when I was twenty-two. It was a bright, sunny summer day, but as my friends and I were walking along the sidewalk, I made the observation that unlike Los Angeles the pavement in Eugene was clean enough that you could lick the sidewalk with your tongue. I proclaimed out loud, "I will never live in a town where it rains so much that the sidewalk pavement is this clean." I ended up spending 30 years living in Eugene, the home of the University of Oregon.

But these two ironies pale next to my eventual discovery that the truth of suffering was accurate. I didn't give The Four Noble Truths much thought until I met Lama Thubten Yeshe in New Zealand when I was twenty-seven. He taught me that friends, family, and all things familiar were only transitory. During an explanation of the Equanimity mind training practice, Lama Yeshe explained that we should treat the three sorts of persons – people who are close to us, those who are our enemies, and those toward whom we have neutral feelings – as equally deserving of our good will. What was the reason for this minimization of the closeness of family, I wondered? I read many Buddhist books during the year after I met Lama Yeshe, and I came across a text in which the Buddha spoke about having to kill your parent, but it was metaphorically explained as a warning not to rely upon the ties of kin because they were impermanent despite seeming to be permanent.

What could be more permanent to a child than his mother? The truth of the impermanence of this seeming permanence was made painfully clear to me when my mother committed suicide after my father left her for a young woman he had been sleeping with secretly for a dozen years. It meant that the illusion of family bliss I had lived when I was a schoolboy was not even real at the time, let alone not permanent. Even worse, my father was so angry at my refusal to bless his new marriage after the suicide that he disowned me. I was left without a family sooner than I had dreamed was possible.

My father spent many years suffering, during which he squandered all of his wealth on this woman, along with gambling and cocaine. Thirty years later – when we had finally reconciled – he had no wealth left to bequeath to anyone. I ended up inheriting his entire estate, which consisted of one envelope filled with postage stamps. That was another irony to behold. In fact I laughed out loud when it happened, delighted with the irony in the way a dancing dakini might be delighted by an encounter with truth. I had no regret whatsoever about losing my inheritance, only remorse for how much both of my parents had suffered, a sentiment that continues to this day. In their lives, which was part of my own life, there truly *was* suffering, and plenty of it; and all of it had a cause, which was desire itself, just as my seventh grade geography textbook had warned me.

But my suffering did not end there, could not end there, for suffering truly is all pervasive. Not only did the family that brought me into the world self-destruct, the family that I myself made as an adult self-destructed. Sometimes I have thought that the young lack the wisdom to know what love really is, or could be, but most of the time I think that I was so inflicted with self-absorption that I just never learned how to love well enough. And so suffering from this lack – each of our lives are experienced as some sort of lack – my wife cheated on me four times. The first two times were so painful for me that my wife thought it prudent to keep me entirely in the dark about her love life thereafter. In the end I was excluded altogether, and for much of the time she lived a secret life unknown to me. After sixteen years, our family – man, woman and son – split up for good. More detailed description of the sufferings of losing these two families is not required here, and I mention it only to offer an illustration of the transitory nature of families, which my lama had tried to explain long ago, even though I was not ready at the time to understand it. Well, the clues had been presented to me when I was twelve, but I was too blinded by youth to recognize them.

Suffering is born from attachments, and those attachments are pervasive. It should be appreciated that an affluent boy from Beverly Hills is not the only person in the world to experience suffering. But suffering also has a cure: let go of the attachments! One can start with the Baskin-Robbins ice-cream cones, but a comprehensive renunciation will take many years of practice, and in a lifetime one can hardly accomplish more than to pare the list down. The more things that are ceded, the greater is the happiness that results. Life is odd in that way.

When I was a new Assistant Professor, my salary was only sufficient to last until the middle of each month. I paid all of the bills on the first of each month, and then we went shopping for this and that. When we ran out of money, the three of us stayed at home. I quickly discovered that the fortnight at home without money was a better time for us than the first fortnight of each month when we still had money. Accordingly, after I was promoted to Associate Professor and reached the stage when my salary was double what I had received at first, instead of spending money all month long and experiencing the mental distractions that the spending of money brings about, I convinced my university to let me return to them one-half of my appointment. That way I received less money but had more time. That way the day when I ran out of money could come sooner in the month, allowing me to be able to sit at home contentedly sooner. A decade after that, when I became a full Professor and my salary increased again, I signed up for an early part-time retirement, and then had nine months free for study and practice and only three months of paid work. Consequently, throughout my career my monthly income has remained flat, while the free time steadily increased. That way, I was able to preserve the time that was available for the real work, leaving me with no more excuses. And no complaints, which may be the best part.

42
India, My Teacher of Patience

Many dharma practitioners, and practitioner imitators like myself, come to India to learn from teachers who still retain some genuine connection to the world of traditional practice. Our thought is that if we meet the right teacher, or receive the right initiation, or maybe if we live in the Himalayas, then we will discover enlightenment. In this fashion we commence one more search for our solutions outside of ourselves, when any real solution is closer at hand, inside us. Tsodruk Rangdrol wrote that we keep following the tracks of the elephant deep into the forest when the elephant we are seeking is already standing right in front of us.

This "quest" and its neurotic urgency has been ridiculed by contemporary Indian observers such as Gita Mehta (*Karma Cola*) and Pankaj Mishra (*Dharma Cola*). But these young Indians underappreciate the resources of their own country's spirituality, so preoccupied are they with their own rejection of the greed and hypocrisy that they have correctly identified in most of India's religious institutions. We arrive in Boudanath, Dharamsala, Kanchipuram, Poona, or Mysore expecting – insisting, really – that we learn the truth from someone else. But truth is not like that. My root lama, Thubten Yeshe, emphasized many times that we have to become our own gurus. My teacher of yoga, Dr. Swami Gitananda, used to say that a real teacher trains not followers but gurus, that is, people who think for themselves.

But how do we learn from India then? More than any ideas from texts or initiations, India itself is the teacher of patience *non pareil*. One can read the brilliant Sixth Chapter of Shantideva's *Entering the Bodhisattva's Way of Life* – one of humanity's finest gems – and still it will have less effect upon the average person than will coping with India for few months.

There is a story about one of the Ch'an patriarchs of Buddhism, who had invited all of the great teachers and practitioners of China to his monastery for a week of study, discussions, and practice. At the end of the week, as one of the participants was about to depart, he complimented the patriarch about the wonderfully productive gathering. He complained only that the patriarch's chef was not at all a good cook and that the meals were wanting. The patriarch replied, "Oh, that man is not my chef! He is my teacher of patience." India is sometimes a teacher of patience.

Westerners, Americans especially, expect things to work. When things do not work – when the electricity is cut, when the propane for the stove is nowhere available, when the matches do not strike in the humidity, when the bus drivers are on a three-day protest, or the bank will not admit their receipt of your telegraphed funds, when both pens and windows leak, when the line at the water pump is two hours long, etc. – Americans become impatient. During the six years I lived in India, I was forced to learn to be patient with life, one-thing-at-a-time. Indian buses were a great teacher. I can now ride anywhere in the only way that Indian buses can be ridden: with all heart-felt desires *abandoned*, I now ride in utter tranquility; instead of worrying about why the driver honks too frequently or drives too recklessly, or takes too many rest stops, etc.... I just go with the flow.

I have a philosophy for coping with India: "If anything can go wrong, it will go wrong." And this aphorism has helped to make life easier for me. Almost to a fault of pride, I can accept my hotel reservations being cancelled, my $200/night room lacking hot water, the announcement of a two-day bandh closing all the shops and halting all travel just prior to my departure, etc., without complaint, even while other Westerners are still arguing the point with the hotel/train/airline manager who is bewildered at how much energy an American is willing to expend upon anger, fruitlessly. For a student of dharma the real teaching is India itself.

Our very first visit to India my wife and I had stayed the three months of our tourist visas, and we loved India so much that we had then exhausted the additional three months that are available by renewal. Since the Government of India is strict about the six-month limit of residence each year, we prepared to depart. But in order to depart we were required to secure a "No Objection to Leave India" certificate from the government. When we went to the office in New Delhi that handled those certificates we were asked to show our encashment receipts, which we received each time that we changed dollars into rupees; this was to ensure that we had not been changing our money on the black market. But no one had told us about our having to save those receipts, and we did not have any of them. We were then informed that we would be unable to leave India. This placed us into a classic double-bind: we were not permitted either to stay or to leave. I pleaded our case, suggesting that we would be willing to do either one, and that the Government of India could make that decision for us, but that obviously one or the other had to be decided. The clerk replied that neither was possible.

Instead of becoming angry or self-righteous, as we might have done in the US, we went over and sat on the couch and waited patiently. We read the novels we had with us until the close of day. The next morning we returned with our novels, made another request and were again refused, and then sat on the couch until the afternoon. It was our idea that all we needed to do was to demonstrate to the clerks that we would not become angry as so many foreign visitors do, maintain a positive attitude, and eventually they would approve our request. In the afternoon the clerk called me to the window and informed me that they would prepare "No Objection" certificates for us. We had demonstrated to them that we could be patient.

Once I spent the better part of the week of the World Congress of Sociology at New Delhi's Taj Hotel, sitting in the lobby observing my fellow sociologists throw fits at the hotel staff who bemusedly observed their behavior. For most of my colleagues it was their first visit to India, but it was too brief to afford them the opportunity to learn any patience. I did not feel disgust nor take pleasure in their plights, but I was interested to watch how they mirrored my own impatience and emotional afflictions. The humor there was not lost on me, however, since I spent many hours laughing in a well-upholstered chair across from the front desk, witnessing capsulized versions of the life I myself have lived in India. The show was so entertaining that I skipped most of the scholars' panel sessions.

India is capable of exposing to me many of my shortcomings, and there are always new occasions to practice, more in India than in my own country. One event I had not yet experienced was a week-long cutoff in mail delivery. For nine days, Sera Monastery did not deliver mail. For a solitary scholar living half-way around the globe, news from home, including my son (then a teenager), from past lovers, etc. can be important. It is easy for mail to become inordinately important. Mail is delivered regularly all over the world. Even in India, the longest gap in mail delivery had only been three days (a Sunday with holidays on both sides). But on this occasion, the monk whose job it was to drive the four miles into town to pick up the mail had gone to Bangalore for a week, and the Sera office did not have a replacement. The staff there was prepared to be content with any situation. After all, that is part of a monk's job. As I once told a visiting friend who was afraid she had just angered one of the monastery's staff persons, "Don't worry about that—not becoming angry is his job."

And this is the point. That is the work I still have to learn. With each passing day without mail delivery, I allowed myself to become increasingly incensed. Just the thought of the mail sitting in bags at the Bylakuppe post office four miles away (or more likely strewn across the tables there as each piece gets inspected for valuable enclosures that can be pilfered) made my blood boil – which was a contribution only to advancing my heart disease. An alternative would have been to welcome the opportunity to go even more deeply into the real work, which is locating that so-called Buddha nature that lurks within. Storming off to the combined offices of Sera Jey and Sera Me (the two monasteries within Sera) in order to identify the lazy, culprit in the matter so I could give him an American-styled well-deserved scolding was *not* the real work. The truth is that they did not care when, or even if, the mail comes.

For the first 17 months that I lived at Sera, I did not have one single argument. Back home, even in sedate Oregon, I can hardly make it as far as lunch without having an argument. There are so many domains of neurotic fixation, and each one can be studied in order to learn where the place from which harmony emanates is located. Finding some calm may be what mantras are for: *Om svabhava shuddha sarva dharma svabhava shuddha hum* ("The nature of my own being is uncontaminated, and so is the nature of all things"). The truth is that even great mantras like this one are only words, and not even a pious comportment while uttering it will improve its efficacy if we do not apply genuine effort. Never mind holy incantations, we need set our sights lower; something more practical like Manipura chakra, the solar plexus. One can cultivate the mantra there.

43
Yoga Tourism in India

It is not a widely known fact, but the famous Swami Vivekananda did not go to the Chicago World Congress of Religions in 1898 for the purpose of proselytizing yoga or vedanta, despite the fact that he was the person who there first introduced yoga to the United States. Most brahmin masters of both of these Hindu traditions bear considerable skepticism about the likelihood of foreigners or non-Hindus achieving substantial spiritual accomplishments. They are open to teaching Westerners, but some of the more traditional among them have expressed the opinion that perhaps the most that an American can hope for is to be reborn as a brahmin, and presumably a male. While their skepticism is myopic, it may not be far from a correct assessment of the result of America's encounters with Hinduism.

The actual aim of Swami Vivekananda's journey to America a century ago was to encourage financial investment in economic projects in India, an aspiration that turned out a century later to be more successful than the propagation in America of *ahimsā*, *aparigraha*, *pratiyahara*, and other fabulous but formidable core practices of Hindu culture. It is for certain that America has bred more capitalists in India than India has been able to foster yogis in America, provided that we hold to a chaste definition of "yogi." This is no fault of Indians, since the American culture of self-satiation does not lend itself naturally to recognizing the shortcomings of *ahamkāra* (the ego-principle).

For most Americans, both in the US and in India, a "yogi" can refer to a person who "does" yoga. And by "yoga" what is usually meant is the practice of *āsana*, the physical positions that compose the third of the eight limbs of yoga, according to Patañjali. Alongside this practice of *āsana*, there may be the suggestion of something spiritual affixed to it, but there is no hard-core religiosity, since most of the Americans who practice yoga (and especially those who have come to India to study it further) have rejected anything that is too regulated or doctrinaire. One must have some independence of mind to begin to adopt cultural practices that are not one's own, and typically, American students of yoga are fiercely independent, original, and relatively self-reliant. If they are sung at all, bhajans are sung for the sake of "feeling nice" and not for their spiritual content. "Meditation" (*dhāranā*) may be attempted, but the five *yama* and five *niyama* are usually not known by their names or meanings, much less practiced. *Pratiyahara*, the cultivation of one's resources for contentment besides what can be provided by the senses, is usually missing altogether.

What is it to "do" yoga? This question has been contemplated by tens of thousands of Americans who now gaze upon the yoga magazines on their supermarket counters. For the vast majority of Americans, "yoga" is a not-too-strenuous way to lose fat effectively and to reduce the stress of a busy life, in that order. For Americans who are not overweight, "doing" yoga involves more strenuous postures that permit one to achieve a slender version of muscularity, become more flexible, firm up the abdomen, and above all, retain a tight butt. Others find their way to what is called "yoga" in order to delay or reverse the onset of arthritis in their joints. Those who keep up a practice of *āsaṇa* for as long as six months express satisfaction with the firmness of their calves and abdomens, and general sense of well-being. The fact that the buttocks really do become tighter motivates additional dedication (if there was doubt about the spiritual benefits of "yoga," the cultivation of tight buttocks overcomes such hesitation). In brief, "yoga" is frequently viewed as a way to become beautiful.

What these motives share is that they are all directed to a notion of yoga *in which the most vital aspects are missing entirely*. Swami Vivekananda would not have recognized it. Nevertheless, quite a few of those Americans who have cultivated a "practice" – usually referred to possessively as "my practice" – find their way to India to secure further instruction at hundreds of centers for teaching "yoga." Few of these centers offer much more than *āsana* and a web-site, although some elementary *prāṇāyāma* may be included. At a number of these establishments a commodification of yoga has taken hold, and ad hoc yoga-tourism industries, actively promoted by local governments and by the Government of India, have bloomed wherever Western (American, European and Latin American) yoga students have gathered. Yoga is for sale, almost exclusively *āsana*, and there are a great many purchasers who come for periods of a few weeks to a few months, and even years if they can secure the visas. The accompanying commodification – yoga mats, yoga bags, yoga shirts, yoga leotards, etc., mostly geared to the practice of *āsana* – is an American modification of yoga, and not part of the original ascetic ideal of a yogi practicing *aparigraha* (abstinence from greed), perhaps living in the forest sitting on an animal skin in *padmāsana*. But ironically it has fulfilled Swami Vivekanada's original dream of encouraging American investment in India.

The typical day of a yoga student in Varanaṣi or Rishikesh, Kovalam or Goa, Mysore or Poona, begins with the student's "practice" of *āsana*, albeit beginning a little too early for most students' preferences (5 or 6 am, but some sacrifice seems appropriate). A few enterprising Indian yoga teachers have learned that there is a solid niche in the yoga market for an 8 am starting time, and they are able to secure more students that way. Following a post-ā*sana* shower, there is usually a large, healthy vegetarian breakfast to be found. This commonly takes place in the dining room or yard of an enterprising Indian housewife, but a number of yoga students themselves have recognized the opening for a more Western-oriented menu, and Westerner owned and operated black market restaurants have appeared spontaneously, which permit the students to fraternize among themselves, uninterrupted by actual people from India. Enterprising Americans ("Are all Americans so enterprising? I wish we Indians were equally enterprising," an Indian housewife once remarked to me) have purchased automatic washing machines and will do yoga students' laundry for a fee, including their yoga mats, relieving students of the opportunity to attempt to communicate with even a *dhobi* (an Indian washer-person), or indeed wash their own clothes by hand the way that most Indians do. American yoga aspirants remain very much inside of their own cultural universe and have minimal contact with Indian society, except for the commodified yoga they desire and receive. They cannot read any signs in the regional language, learn little about the politics or culture ("We're only here for a few months"), and keep their focus upon their own practice of ā*sana*. The most appalling part of it is that many of them suffer from a smugness that is derived from their having completed so fine an advanced practice of ā*sana* early in the morning, entitling them to spend the rest of the day in idleness while bearing a feeling of superiority toward most of the people they meet during the day. This has produced an odd sort of "yogi."

Following the breakfast, many yoga students head off into "town" or "city" for shopping and generally end up at a four or five-star hotel's swimming pool where they rendezvous with their fellow practitioners and encounter only the few smiling but sycophantic Indians who work on the hotel's staff. The pool-sides are not all that different from the pool-sides in their own back yards in America, and one wonders what kind of seekers would try to duplicate the identical milieu they already know. By their own reports, many of them did come on a quest of sorts, but they get misguided by those Western yoga tourists who have preceded them and who quickly school them in the routines for deriving amusement from the Indian locality. Insulated by a critical mass of like-minded pleasure-seekers, they are socialized quickly to a mild hedonism, which unnecessarily limits their opportunities for discovering India; instead, they invest a good deal of their energies shopping, a skill at which they are already masters.

It can be said without cynicism that Americans are brilliant at shopping, and India offers quality and bargains that cannot be obtained in the US. The same brand-name clothing that Indians ship to the US is available on the Indian market for a fraction of its US cost. The cotton and silk garments are luxurious, and woolen shawls and sweaters are rich, natural, and sold for less than what a second-hand store in the US would sell them for. CDs of the latest world music are available for $2 each, and a fabulous array of Indian classical music is also available. India is the world's second largest publisher of books in English, and they sell them for a tenth of what an American publisher charges. Woodcrafts, beauty oils, soaps, jewelry, brass items, the list of inexpensive items available keeps the "yoga" students' heads spinning, and the satisfaction of acquiring so much for so little money leaves the students convinced that they are living fruitful days. But is that satisfaction a healthy thing, at least for a yogi who should be practicing abstinence from greed instead of coveting everything that is spread out before one and within one's grasp?

What is troubling about this is that the students are building *vāsanā* – habitual, automatic mind-energy patterns – for doing even *more* shopping, and it is not difficult to imagine that this *vāsanā* will continue to operate after they return to the West, rendering their trip to India a failure by any yogic standard. It is not difficult to encounter Western yogis who are shopping animals, ravenous for yet another bargain-filled outing. For Westerners with modest incomes, it is as if they have become rich at last. The problem here is not that they acquired a good book at a low cost, but that they have developed not more, but less, ability to be satisfied with few possessions (the practice of *santosha*, during which one learns to be responsible for one's own contentment, without any props) – an accomplishment that will endlessly enrich their lives and that can serve as the basis for a real practice of yoga. That is why *santosha* and *aparigraha* belong to the *niyama* and *yama* (respectively) and are placed at *the beginning* of a yogi's quest. Ask most students of yoga what is the meaning of *aparigraha*, and most will not be able to offer a response. This is rendered more pathetic by considering that a majority of these yoga tourists are yoga teachers in the West.

After the shopping comes the poolside activities – swimming, sun-tanning, and reading (which mostly consists of gossiping with friends while holding a book in one's hand). A few yoga centers offer some afternoon classes or "*satsangh*," but only a minority of Western yoga students choose to attend them, preferring to attend the "anti-*satsangh*" of their poolside banter, or perhaps preferring the suntan itself. When challenged about the wisdom of their selection, they typically mutter something about being "so tired" from waking up at such an early hour. While some impromptu classes are offered by an ad hoc yoga tourism industry (including Indian cooking, Ayurvedic massage, Sanskrit, etc.), the Indian teachers of these classes, mostly ordinary householders, nearly always report surprise and dismay over the lack of responsibility many yoga students display by not showing up at classes for which they have registered, skipping classes (in favor of the pool or party), or leaving town inadvertently forgetting to pay balances due for services rendered (insignificant to them but significant to most Indians). "One expects more from yoga students!" is the exhasperated lament I have heard most frequently from Indians.

Even book-reading is kept to a minimum, and most serious texts that elucidate the thought of Vedanta, Buddhism or Jainism are considered to be "too heady." That is because many of the people who are attracted to yoga are anti-intellectual. The strategy of using the body and one's 72,000 nerves in skillful ways to produce harmony – which is surely the genius of yoga – attracts many persons who have mostly rejected analytic strategies. Yes, we have bodies, but the point is to use them to gain more control over the mind, for the object of a practice of yoga is to control the mind. In *Vivekachudamani* (which some attribute to Shankara) the sage himself cautions against "book-knowledge," and yet Shankara is tendering this advice in a book. While the *Chāndogya Upanishad* asserts, "If speech were not there, there would be no knowledge of virtue, truth and falsehood, good and bad, pleasant and unpleasant. Surely speech makes all this known." Yet Swami Sivanada argues correctly that since *samādhi* is "beyond the reach of speech and mind, you will have to realize this yourself." Hence, the study of texts is a necessary but insufficient part of *swadhaya* (self-study), yet most yoga tourists skip the text study part, while offering glib anti-intellectual cants about the shallowness of words and the need for "actual practice." Yes, one expects more from people who will teach yoga.

Phrased differently, Hatha Yoga attracts participants in the tens (and even hundreds) of thousands, whereas Raja Yoga attracts hardly dozens. One time during a visit to a Sanskrit university in Tamil Nadu, a curious stranger asked me "what kind of yoga" my teacher Swami Gitananda taught. I replied, "hatha yoga." Unfortunately for me, Swamiji overheard me, and it was the only time that Swamiji ever became furious with me. He would not speak to me for the remainder of that day, commenting only that he "never" teaches Hatha Yoga. (Actually, he taught it rarely.) The next day I asked Swamiji what my answer should have been, and he replied "Ashtanga Yoga."

By "Ashtanga" Swamiji meant *all* eight limbs of Patañjali's yoga. How emblematic it is of the problem facing American yoga that in America "Ashtanga Yoga," is known widely as a highly athletic form of *āsana* practice involving *vinyāsa* (a form of athleticism) and regulated breathing. It is a brilliant method of *āsana*, but most Americans are unaware of the correct meaning of "*ashtanga*." America has reinvented yoga in ways that are more compatible with its commodified, pleasure-seeking culture.

While at the five-star hotel in the afternoon, American yoga students also find beer and wine, and other alcoholic beverages. One sign at a yoga center publicized "Alcoholics Anonymous for Yogis." It was not a joke. And non-vegetarian meals are the rule rather than the exception. The sterility of the social ambience of a five-star hotel is compensated somewhat by the relief of its air conditioning. The real India may be waiting for the students a block away, but for the afternoon it can remain out-of-mind.

It may be said objectively that the main preoccupation of Western "yogis" in India is courtship. Romantic love has its place. Loneliness is not to be praised, and sexuality itself is to be celebrated. However, the average Westerner's residence in India of three months' duration is marked most prominently by the high of a new love affair and the pain of its demise, often as the fallout of the entry of a third party and yet an additional affair. That would be alright if such experience would teach a lesson in false expectations and the projection of fantasies, but more commonly the disappointment is solved by cultivating a subsequent affair, until the day for leaving India finally arrives. Romantic partnership is legitimate, but so is yoga, which comes to play a bit part during the Indian sojourn, even though it may have motivated the journey. Whatever may be the value of such courtship, it is not exactly what the rishis had in mind when they placed *bramacharya* on the list of *yama*.

Any day prior to a person's departure from India is genuine grounds for a "yoga party." I'm not making this up. Since these tourists are always arriving and departing, such parties occur most of the time. Just which yogi is it who is searching for a party? If no one happens to be leaving, it may be someone's birthday. If there are two hundred yoga students in town, then there can be a birthday party on most days, certainly weekly. And the relative visibility of one's birthday party becomes a sort of de facto measurement of one's standing on the local social scale. Behold: the American yogis have successfully reproduced in India the social structure of their high school experience. What is difficult is to find a period of time that is without a party. One needs only interview the staff of the local Indian police station to collect the details, which include noise complaints and some drug usage.

So that is the yogi's typical day in India. I must confess to the reader that I know so much about it because I am one of those who surrendered to the decadent lifestyle I am describing. Naturally, it is the morning "practice" that ennobles the lifestyle, and it is that practice by which a yoga sadakh may be judged. Of what precisely does the practice on which yoga tourists retain their focus consist? Young people seeking fitness, older people wanting to regain youth (most of them self-absorbed with a focused effort to become or remain attractive) focus their energies intently upon what each one of them term "my practice." For one or two hours they direct their energies (and in many cases this energy is abundant and highly directed) upon themselves. Only themselves. Each breath is a celebration of one's body electric. It may be beautiful, but the danger is that it can reinforce egotism and self-centeredness at the very time that one's practice of yoga should be eradicating the self, egoistically conceived. In all fairness, it may be said that a yoga practitioner will inevitably meet other practitioners who are more adept at ā*sana* or run up against the limits of his or her body. But a sense of inadequacy is not actually the opposite of egoism, since it can be just another form of self-absorption. If Patañjali is to be believed, spiritual lessons can be gained from a correct practice of ā*sana*, but when the practice is distorted by what is already most abundant in the culture – vanity, pleasure-seeking, and self-absorption – is there a fair chance for its cultivation? The metaphor of the camel that is unable to pass through the eye of the needle seems appropriate here.

One longtime friend of mine, the Western Geshe Michael Roach, was undertaking a three-year meditative retreat, and he decided that he and his fellow retreatants could benefit from some physical mind-body activity, and he invited a senior instructor of Ashtanga Yoga to the retreat to teach the meditators the basic sequence of ā*sana*. After practicing this method for some time, my friend began to be disturbed by his observation that with each breath, more "self" cultivation was being practiced. Instead of developing a mind that tended towards thinking about the needs of others – the purpose of the retreat – the practice of yoga ā*sana* drew him and his party to think more about themselves. He devised a technique to remedy the problem: with each slow inhalation he visualized taking upon himself the suffering and pain of others, and with each slow exhalation, timed with their movement into and out of the poses, he imagined offering to these suffering fellow beings a healing, consoling energy. In this way, with each breath he was able to redirect his mental focus away from "my practice" to a practice of the Giving-Taking Meditation that could sustain the cultivation of a concern for others.

This method is more consistent with a genuine practice of yoga. And what is yoga, properly conceived, one may want to ask? Yoga is learning to direct one's heart and mind to identifying the *vāsanā sana* (habitual, characterological energy patterns) that pollute one's experience and that continue to taint oneself and others with gross, selfish, short-sighted thoughts, and then reducing or removing those *vāsanā* so identified. Yoga is evolution. Or, as Swami Gitananda once said, "The meaning of life is to evolve. Unfortunately, most of us are preoccupied with devolving."

That seems an apt way to sum up the sojourn of most Western yoga seekers in India. It is not really India's fault – they could never have anticipated how powerful and resilient could be the commodification of everything accomplished by American culture (now practiced throughout the world) nor how effortlessly it could reduce the spiritual resources of yoga to more of the same. Swami Vivekananda himself could not have known. But if he could, it is my guess that he would not have gone to Chicago and would have remained in India, concentrating on his own culture's chances to put the practices of yoga to use in meaningful evolution.

44
Transforming Illness Into the Path

I conclude this volume with a radical suggestion, which may sounds ridiculous at first, but it is meant seriously: if you can come close to death without actually dying, I recommend it, since it will transform the rest of your life. Even if you do not face a life-jeopardizing situation, it may be possible to learn from the experience of those who have. Let me explain.

Members of my family have a congenital defect of the aortic valve, whereby what is normally a tricuspid valve at the outgoing "door" for the blood exiting the heart is for us a bicuspid valve, for the reason that two of the three "flaps" at the valve are fused at birth. Other than rendering us short-winded due to the way it reduces the efficiency of blood circulation, it does not become dangerous until we reach fifty years of age, when a lifetime of calcium gradually accreting at the flaps makes the fused cusped so heavy that it eventually rips off. Many of my ancestors did not live past 50, which was not unusual centuries ago.

The result of this congenital heart defect is that the heart is eventually unable to pump blood normally – what blood exits the aorta keeps re-entering it (this is called regurgitation), requiring that it be pumped again, endlessly; moreover, without the suction of a closed aortic valve, there is much less propulsion to the blood that does flow. The result is that the heart's atrium muscle has to push harder, and the heart muscle gradually increases until it has doubled in size, for the reason that during the later stages of this malady the muscle must pushing the blood through the body without the benefit of a valve. In the end, serious pain and damage occur, ultimately resulting in death. This in fact was the malady that ended the life of my root lama, Thubten Yeshe.

In my family, my mother, aunt, brother, son, some cousins and myself have this defect. As best we can figure, it is the result of too many of our Italian ancestors marrying their cousins, as was common among the nobility of Europe during the 16th to 19th centuries (our family counts princes and princesses among our number, probably titles that were related to the conquests that our Norman ancestors made in southern Italy in the 11th century at the end of the Crusades). I was oblivious to the problem until my doctor first heard the murmur in my mid-forties, and his diagnosis came as a shock to me. It explained at once why the sports I was best at were the short-burst types, such as football, baseball, and the hundred-yard dash (think "crusader"), whereas I was always poor at any sport that required endurance, like basketball, swimming, or long-distance running. The cardiologist told me that one day soon I would reach a point where the heart would rapidly fail, and then I would require surgery.

For three decades my office was on the eighth floor, and much of that time I climbed the stairs for the exercise (I also used to slide down the bannisters for all eight floors, half-floor by half-floor, with my briefcase). One autumn, I found myself unable to make the climb without becoming dizzy ("syncope"), and at age 51 it was time for me to visit the cardiologist. An appointment was made for me with an echocardiologist at the hospital, which was less than a mile from my home in Eugene, Oregon, and a kind and able technician administered the sonar probes that displayed a television-like view of my heart. After some ten minutes of examination, the technician calculated some ratios, jumped up in alarm, told me to remain lying on the table, and ran out the door to find the cardiologist. She returned five minutes later with the news that the doctor had left for the day, since it was already past 5 pm.

"What's the problem?" I asked her.

"I'm sorry. I don't have the authority to discuss it with you," she replied.

With some concern I asked her, "Well I'm sorry, too, but you can't be acting like this. It's not fair to me. What's going on?"

"All I can tell you is that you must return first thing in the morning, and be prepared to have surgery in case it is necessary."

I collected my things and skateboarded home. When I walked in the door, my son was having his afternoon nap on the living room couch, and he awoke. He asked me at once, "How did the test go?" I replied: "I flunked."

"What do you mean?" he asked.

"I don't know, they won't tell me. But I have to return in the morning, and I may need to have surgery." My son rose from the couch, came up to me, and gave me a hug, from which he was unwilling to let go for five full minutes. I admit that they were the best five minutes of my life.

After dinner I decided that I did not think I was ill enough to have surgery, and that I would resist any order for an operation. Not only did I have the final four weeks of the academic term to deal with, the most critical period for my students, I did not trust such a serious surgery. The next morning when I spoke with the cardiologist, I told him about my decision. He replied, "Well, there is no question that it is time for you to have surgery. You will do irreversible damage to your heart without a new valve. But I think we have about three weeks before the situation becomes urgent, and we even can try for four weeks if you like, since you live so close to the hospital."

I left his office determined never to have the surgery, much like Lama Yeshe had decided. During the next four weeks I became increasingly out of breath. I had to stop skateboarding and also I ceased to climb the eight floors to my office. In fact, I was becoming alarmed with my syncope and began to second-guess my decision to refuse the surgery. By the beginning of the fourth week, when the doctor called to confirm the operation he had scheduled, I was scared of dying – I had become so uncomfortable that I had become eager to have the surgery.

It was a difficult surgery, during which they replaced my defective valve with the reconstructed valve of a pig, and I had never known such pain. It seems that my heart had fallen into spasms while I was on the heart-lung machine, and the doctors were afraid that they would be unable to get my heart restarted. During that time the heart-lung machine was unable to supply sufficient oxygen to my brain, and I suffered some minor brain damage, to the extent that I could not think well or concentrate sufficiently enough for the tasks I was looking forward to completing during the months of free time I was expecting following the surgery. Since my surgery had entitled me to a term of paid sick leave, I had planned at last to begin writing my *magnum opus*, a long ethnographic study of Tibetan philosophical debating. It was the research in which I had most heavily invested myself, more than a decade, and at last I was ready to "write it up".[16]

Instead of doing some major writing, I found myself barely capable of reading a newspaper. We even secured a television for the living room, and I realized I had really "lost it" when I found myself unable to follow the twists of the plot to a Dean Martin and Jerry Lewis movie. My assessment was that some minor cell damage had stalled the movement of nerve signals across the usual circuits. Gradually, my brain recruited new pathways for sending messages, but it was six months before I returned to normal. Having skipped the winter term, I taught half time during the spring term, and I found myself barely able to keep up. By the succeeding fall, however, I had returned to normal, although not a page of my book had been written.

---

16 Kenneth Liberman, *Dialectical Practice in Tibetan Philosophical Culture: An Ethnomethodological Inquiry Into Formal Reasoning*, Lanham, Maryland: Rowman & Littlefield, 2004. Paper edition 2007.

Our office secretaries complimented me for my having become more patient and more gentle, the result of my no longer becoming upset about small matters.

What I wish most to relate about this first of my open-heart surgeries is the story of "The Six Week Visit" to the heart surgeon, so that he could check on the final results of his surgery. It was during this visit that he removed by suction two liters of seepage from the heart that had collected at the bottom of my bowels. I spent more than an hour sitting in the waiting room, surrounded by a half dozen heart patients upon which the surgeon had operated the same week as me, and I took the opportunity to study them. None of them seemed to be in good spirits.

On the other hand, I was feeling a great deal of calm. Somehow, coming so close to dying had caused most of the unimportant annoyances to evaporate from my life. I no longer sweated small things, and I felt that I had instantly gained better perspective upon what really mattered in life. My principal concern was whether my newly found harmony and wise judgment would endure, or whether it would fade away as soon as I began to reinvest myself in the ephemeral affairs of living. The surgery had taught me that much of what I took to be important was not nearly so important as I imagined, and I experienced a feeling of being liberated.

To my surprise, that was not the experience of the other patients in the waiting room. All of them older than me, their suffering was palpable. They even seemed bitter. After nearly half an hour had passed I decided to make a comment to the group: "I never imagined how painful this operation turned out to be." They all groaned in unison and endorsed my sentiment. One of them cussed, others shook their heads, and one man said, "I'll never let them do this to me again!" I had caused a good deal of pent-up anger to be released, and once it was in the air the patients just piled it on. Another patient declared that he had done nothing to deserve so much pain and suffering, and the others nodded in agreement. They had had responses to the surgery that differed from mine: instead of feeling liberated by this opportunity to have the mortality of their lives confront them, they had built up resentment about it. Instead of it helping their spiritual lives, they had become paralyzed by their own anger; moreover, they seemed to think that the world now owed them something.

Was it the pain that we all had experienced that had made them so bitter, I wondered? But the task of enduring pain is a universal burden that we share with all living creatures. It is part of our living, and for a human being at least, learning how to cope with pain is a major life task; it may even be an obligation that we owe to humanity: learning how to not permit pain to reduce our kindness. Surely, if we could use it to *increase* our wisdom and compassion, that would be a Buddhist path. While I had found the pain at times overwhelming, I also discovered that pain can wipe out all of one's petty preoccupations as quickly as one shakes an Etch-a-sketch. And when the pain subsides, one is left more "clean-clear" than before. Lama Yeshe used to use the term "clean-clear" to stand for the basic lucidity of the mind that is its fundamental nature, before our personal self-identification even, as explained in many texts on Mahamudra. It is the mind's default state, to which it returns when the more ephemeral conceptual structures are lost for any reason, or fall away. How could it be that the relative clarity to which the pain that my fellow patients had suffered, as I did, had not resulted in their being *less* invested in resentment, pettiness, and anger?

Oh, how sad it made me to witness it! If they had passed up this excellent opportunity for learning about life, what likelihood was there that they would they ever gain spiritual insight? I resolved to never loosen my hold upon what I had learned. I described what had occurred in the waiting room to my surgeon, and he told me that it was common for patients to became embittered.

As the months passed, I lost my hold. Despite my resolve to retain my new perspective, by the time a year had passed I had become pretty much my same old petty self. I recognized that I had lost that unique perspective, and regretted it, but it was difficult for me to regenerate the insight I had held so close to me during the months that followed that first surgery. It was unfortunate.

By the time I reached my mid-fifties I had nearly forgotten that I had a pig valve. I returned to my yoga, running, surfing, and mountain climbing; and I mistook what was really only an interval between heart surgeries for the solution to my heart problems. After four years, I recommenced my travels, began teaching in Italy, Brazil, China, and finally returned to India. It had always been my policy in India to suspend my irregular practice of dental flossing, out of fear of contaminating my system with bacteria from my fingers, which can cause dysentery. When I returned to Eugene, my fabulous dentist became upset with me about the state of my gums. He told me, "Ken, you are a walking time bomb. You have a pig valve, which is vulnerable to infection, and your gums are breeding oral bacteria that have the ability to infect you. You need to begin to floss regularly."

Genuinely afraid, I purchased five kinds and multiple flavors of dental floss and dental tape, took them home and began to floss each night. The flossing turned my gums into bleeding open sores. I complained to my dentist, but he said that after a fortnight the gums would begin to heal. I said to him, "Each time I come for a teeth cleaning I need to take antibiotics to protect my artificial valve, but I bleed more when I floss! Am I supposed to take antibiotics permanently?" He mentioned something about there being a difference of opinion about taking precautionary antibiotics, and so I left them aside when I flossed, even though for a fortnight my gums kept bleeding each time.

After a few weeks, my gums had healed and no longer bled. I was astonished at the capacity of the body to heal itself. I continued to floss, and my oral hygiene improved; however, I contracted a persistent cough – about one cough each minute – and the cough would not go away. After a month of coughing it was gradually driving me mad, and I went to see a pulmonary specialist, who told me that I had probably contracted a mild case of the whooping cough that had been going around; he assured me that my cough would gradually clear up. The pulmonary doctor was like the man who was looking for the key in Thubten Chodren-la's "Introduction" to this book: the doctor sought his diagnosis only within the realm of diseases that were his medical expertise, like looking for the key under the lamplight even though the lamp is on the wrong side of the street.

As the weeks passed, I returned to my home in Baja California, but the cough persisted. What was worse was that I started feeling weak and began sleeping 12 hours a day. I had about two or three clear-headed hours each morning, with which I chose to invest in my daily surfing, and then fell into a soporific daze for the remainder of the day. One morning I returned to bed right after the hot shower that follows my surf session, and I commenced shivering for several hours while I fell in and out of napping. I became scared because I had piled about seven blankets on top of me, but I could not become warm. It took an hour to will myself out of bed and into the kitchen to boil some hot water, which finally ended my shivering, after which I went back to bed. Two days later I had a stroke, which paralyzed my right leg for many days. Witnessing my limp, one of my neighbors, a retired doctor, came up to me to tell me, "Ken, I've been watching you these last few weeks. I do not know what is ailing you, but whatever it is it is systemic, and it will kill you in another month if you do not go up to the States and obtain proper medical attention." I recognized the truth of what he said and that afternoon packed up my car, and I drove up to San Diego the next morning.

I visited a cardiologist, the first I'd seen in several years. He identified some atrial fibrillation, gave me some digitalis, and suddenly I felt better. The cough stopped – it appears that due to my heart's irregular breathing for nearly three months the blood was backing up in the atrium and leaking onto my lungs, whereupon I had to cough to clear out the lungs. It also accounted for my mild stroke, since some of the blood had coagulated for the several minutes that it resided in the atrium before exiting the aorta and entering my blood vessels. The cardiologist told me that my regimen of daily aspirin had probably spared me from experiencing permanent brain damage.

He had done a blood test, which was negative, and he told me that since I had no further problems I would feel better soon. I was still sleeping 12-14 hours a day, so he prohibited me from returning to my home in Baja, he wanted to keep an eye on me, but he kept insisting that I was in recuperation. I spent three weeks in San Diego, and initially I kept surfing each morning. When I nearly passed out from dizziness on a day of eight-foot waves, I resolved – right out there in the lineup – to stop surfing; after taking that last big wave in, a wonderful wave despite the circumstances, I drove straight to the cardiologist, inquiring, "Doc, if I'm getting better then why am I dying?"

I searched for an internal medicine specialist and found an excellent one. He ran every test he could. Several blood tests came back negative, as the first test had been, but this specialist would not take negative for an answer, and he kept the pressure on the lab to keep the blood culture alive, even beyond the usual ten day maximum. My son flew out from Washington, D.C., in order to spend the New Year's weekend with me at our Baja home, and my cardiologist had given me permission to go to my home in Baja California for the long weekend. I was now sleeping nearly 15 hours each evening.

The night before we were to drive the five hours to our Baja home, I developed a fever during the night, and it was then that I knew: I must have bacterial endocarditis. In my delirium we packed the car for Baja anyway, but as we passed by the freeway exit for my specialist's office, I said to my son, "I think I'll stop by my doctor's and inform him that I have a fever." When I walked into the doctor's office, he spotted me and shouted, "Ken! I've been trying to reach you for two days!" I had been up in Los Angeles collecting my son from the airport.

I instantly said to him, "Don't speak. Let me tell *you*. I have bacterial endocarditis, and I have to go to the hospital at once." He nodded yes, that was exactly it. The lab technicians had finally got my blood culture to show bacteria; however, they were unable to identify which bacteria it was.

I entered the hospital, and for the next three days my fever grew in intensity, and I became delirious. The hospital staff had no luck in identifying the bacteria either. As my son sat next to me in the hospital room, I was gradually giving up hope of surviving. They had been administering a broad-based antibiotic, which had no effect. On the fourth day I told my son, "This is going to end soon, one way or the other. I don't have any more fight left in me. Either they will identify the bacteria and cure me, or I will die. Either way it will end soon."

"Don't talk that way," my son replied.

"No, you need to prepare yourself," I said. "Don't worry, I have no regrets. I have had time while I have been laying here to review my entire lifetime, and I have not identified a single important decision or thing that I would change. It has been a fabulous life. You will be fortunate if you are able to live a life as interesting and without regret as mine has been." I felt much contentment. I was ready to die, and I felt no desperation whatsoever. On the contrary, having finally let go of everything, I experienced an enduring sense of peace. I even smiled.

I told my son, "They'll probably figure this thing out, but there is a chance I will die. Don't worry, I am completely at peace." I recalled what one of my best friends said to me when he was at his home days away from dying of lung cancer; he said to me, "It's funny, it's as if we humans are programmed to die. I feel no unhappiness about it at all." But my son did not want me to be thinking that way.

During that night, the lab technicians correctly identified the bacteria that had been causing my problems:

Cardiobacterium hominis. They told me that it was a common bacteria that resided harmlessly in many people's mouths. With a name like that it surprised me that it was not Bacterial Suspect Number One. Somehow it had contaminated the site of my aortic valve, which was vulnerable to infection since it was a laboratory-produced artifact and receives no blood itself, despite being the passageway through which all the blood passes. Surely the bacteria had entered my blood system during the fortnight that my gums were bleeding from flossing. They sent the hospital dentist to examine me, and he advised me, "There are three ways to floss: never, always, or once in a while. The last one is the most dangerous, and that is the way that you have been flossing."

He also told me that this bacteria was so benign and slow growing that it repeatedly failed to develop when cultured; nevertheless, it had slowly colonized the valve site and then bred throughout my body, turning me septic. They switched to the correct antibiotic, and 36 hours later it was as if I had awakened from a decades-long sleep, just like Rip Van Winckle.

Two days later I was sitting up in the lotus position on my bed, meditating and answering emails on my laptop. On the third day I asked the nurse, "Since I'm now cured, how long will it be before I can go home to Baja?" She replied, "Go home? Who said anything about going home? As soon as your body is free of the bacteria, we are transferring you to the main hospital where you will have open-heart surgery to replace your valve. Didn't the doctor tell you?" This was not good news.

This second open-heart surgery was easier than the first one was, even though the surgeon took more than six hours to scrape off the contaminated tissue at the valve site and replace the pig valve with a bovine valve. The cardiac nurses explained to me that the heart-lung machines had improved a great deal in the six years since my previous surgery. Of course there was still much pain, and my body was devastated. Again, it took more than a year for me to regain the level of health and fitness that I had before the infection. Since my brain was not damaged this time, during my recovery months I began reading Proust's six-volume *Researching Lost Time*, and my mood was quite good. I never became depressed. In fact, I have not had a moment of depression or an unhappy day in the eight years following. It seems that this time the new perspective that such a life-threatening situation is able to provide has been more durable. I attribute this to the fact that when I was so near to dying, I had let go of everything so completely.

Now each day is like a "freebee" for me, and so there is reason to celebrate every day. I have become carefree and pratically unflappable, even buoyant. It was not really any of my wide reading in philosophy or sociology that caused this, nor the efforts I made over the years to practice Buddhism successfully. It was the contingency of dying, and then of surviving, that led me to this transformation of my orientation. I was not the agent for it; if anything, it came as a surprise to me. I had let go because I recognized in a direct and non-conceptual way that the ego in which I had for decades been investing my energy amounted to nothing. For a moment I had witnessed the flow of being itself, and my individuation of it was no important matter.

It was a spiritual realization to be sure, but nothing that I had a direct hand in. During my recovery, I wrote the following poem:

*Shunyashunya**

Shaken at the end of the solstice,
but the ghost wouldn't give itself up.
Everything else did, though —
the fever shook loose most of my objectives;
self-conceits were shed first,
followed by projects picked up
for no better purpose than amusement;
it was good to lose the distractions.

Once the infection and fever were cured,
the heart surgery could follow.
It was then that the foundation stones of career
and identity were surrendered also.
Memories long forgotten,
the signposts of a life soon to be lost,
rushed in to fill the spaces,
and then they too were cut loose.

By the end, [I] was hardly there,
practically mere being,
without the encumbrances of purpose
and self. Friends and relatives shrank
as if they lived at the wrong end of binoculars.
Every idea seemed artificial.

What is this ghost that remains,
more nothing than something?

A fortnight of postoperative pain,
syncope and fibrillation
rendered even this question null.
There remained only a capacity to survive,
which was in no way voluntary
but a slow engine
that ran under its own momentum.

I learned again how to sleep on my stomach,
how to walk, bend, lift; in time,
I could risk to laugh, and to sneeze.
As the waxing days of late winter came,
I began to reappropriate my identity
as one might walk into the closet
to regard one's wardrobe
and fit one's nothing-something
into familiar pants and jackets.
Though these identities struck me
as so much artifice,

as the weeks progressed
they became more convincing.

My daily walks lengthen
with the gaining sunlight.
I choose primitive canyons,
ignored and hidden between the mesas
of San Diego's cultureless megalopolis.
The season's new warmth stirs me into life,
and much like a butterfly
that has just crawled out of its cocoon
and readies to stretch out one of its wings,
I reclaim a life both estranged and recognizable.

* *shunyashunya*= "nothing-something" (Sanskrit)

I walked every day, and after eight months I felt my chest was well healed enough to begin running again. By the end of the first year I recommenced surfing; however, I experienced much difficulty breathing. After two years, I was still unable to run a mile or paddle without becoming dizzy, and so I sought help from my cardiologist, who sent me to an electrocardiologist who dealt with heart arrhythmias. He concluded that in the effort to cut out all of the infected tissue, the surgeon had cut my atrial/ ventricular node, and it was no longer transmitting the signals to my heart that indicate when it should beat. Any time that my heart exceeded about 90 beats per minute, it fell into a basal rhythm of about 30 beats per minute: think the cartoon character "Road-runner" spinning his wheels while suspended a few feet off of the cliff just before he falls and crashes. I could not blame the surgeon, since he had a difficult task to face: if he did not cut enough, the bacteria would have reinfected me; and if he had cut too much, he would have had to replace the entire aorta with the artificial aorta that he kept beside him throughout the long surgery. Just thinking of him bent over for six hours, made me sympathetic to him; and he had saved my life.

So I had a surgery to implant a pacemaker, which made necessary another period of rest, recuperation, and recovery. But even two years later, there was little improvement to my circulation. Either the wires had not taken well, or I had tugged one of them out while doing some yoga *āsana*, I'll never know. Yet another pacemaker operation was needed, and this time they placed two wires into the heart. Since the earlier wire would not come out without tearing a hole in the atrium, I now have three wires running from my shoulder to my heart, which makes for a great deal of congestion and affects my upper body's flexibility. After four heart operations in all, I am able to surf once more, but I am still usually made breathless by my heart's inability to crank out sufficient blood at peak exertion. I think they have designed these pacemakers for geriatrics and not for athletes like myself. Well, I don't mind slowing down some. Since I am past 65 years, it is about time anyway. The pleasure I derive from riding even a single wave now is as great as what a dozen used to offer me forty years ago. Again, no complaints.

Maybe this is the only dharma practice I have accomplished – I don't complain. I have won a special perspective. I find joy everywhere I gaze, and hold on protectively to nearly nothing. *Everyone* should try it. I would offer the additional advice not to actually die, but I don't think that part is possible.